WRONG TURNS, RIGHT LESSONS

Lessons from an Imperfect Life

COPYRIGHT © 2025 KSHAMA SINGHI

All rights reserved. No part of this book may be reproduced, stored in a retrieval system, or transmitted in any form or by any means—electronic, mechanical, photocopying, recording, or otherwise—without prior written permission from the author, except for brief quotations in reviews or articles.

This book is a work of personal experience and reflection. While every effort has been made to ensure accuracy, the author makes no representations or warranties regarding the content's completeness, reliability, or suitability.

DISCLAIMER

This book is intended for informational and inspirational purposes only and does not constitute professional advice. The insights shared are based on the author's personal journey and coaching experiences. They should not replace therapy, legal, medical, or financial advice from qualified professionals. Readers are encouraged to seek professional guidance for their specific circumstances.

The author and publisher disclaim any liability for any loss or damage resulting from using the information provided in this book. Each reader is responsible for their own choices and actions.

For permissions, inquiries, or to connect with the author, please visit: **WWW.COACHKSHAMA.COM**

DEDICATED TO

This book is for all the women who have lived their lives carrying the weight of society's expectations, only to wake up one day feeling an ache of regret or resentment for the dreams they set aside. It is for the women who have quietly believed themselves to be less than others, who grew up feeling invisible, unheard, and convinced they were not enough. It is for the women who have been forced into roles and stereotypes, confined to moulds that never reflected their true, vibrant essence.

To the women who have felt betrayed by a world that demanded they shrink themselves to fit in, who have had to suppress their dreams, voices, and truth to survive—this book is for you. It is for the women who have poured their hearts into being the perfect daughter, sister, wife, or mother, only to lose sight of who they truly are, and for those who now stand bravely at the edge of rediscovery, ready to reclaim themselves.

This is a tribute to your quiet tears and unseen battles, resilience in the face of heartbreak, and courage to rise again. May this book hold space for your pain, ignite the fire of self-belief, and remind you that you are never alone. You are worthy, powerful, and enough; within you lies the strength to rewrite your story.

FOREWORD

There comes a time in life when you must confront the stories you tell yourself —those that shape your relationships, self-worth, and future. For many, this realisation comes after heartbreak, adversity, or a major life transition. In these moments, you have a choice: to stay stuck in pain or to reclaim your power and rewrite your story.

Kshama Singhi's journey is one of profound transformation. From enduring loneliness and self-doubt to rediscovering her worth and purpose, she has emerged not just as a survivor but as a guide for others seeking healing and empowerment. In these pages, she shares her experiences with honesty and courage, offering a story of resilience and a roadmap for reclaiming your life.

This book is more than inspiration—it's an invitation to step into your strength, break free from limiting beliefs, and create a life filled with meaning. No matter where you are on your journey, *Kshama's* words will remind you that you have the power to heal, grow, and thrive. Your story is still being written. Let this book help you turn the page.

With admiration,
Vishal Morjaria

ACKNOWLEDGEMENT

First and foremost, I want to express my deepest gratitude to my late papa, who instilled in me the values that have guided my life. Your wisdom has been the foundation upon which I've built everything. To my mum, from whom I inherited the strength and the indomitable spirit to keep fighting, thank you for showing me the power of resilience and perseverance.

To my daughter, who became the inspiration that transformed my life, you are my light and my motivation. Every step of this journey has been for you, and your presence has pushed me to strive for the best version of myself.

I want to acknowledge my sisters Tapasya and Namrata for trusting me as their coach and presenting challenges that revealed my true potential in this role. I also want to acknowledge my brother Pranav, my sister-in-law Sona, and my friends Punya and Irina. Your unwavering support and the sense of security you've provided have been my rock. The love and unity of our family have given me the courage to pursue my dreams.

Special thanks go to Rujuta Diwekar and Jinal Shah, who introduced me to a different lifestyle and helped me redefine my relationship with food. Your guidance transformed my physical health and contributed immensely to my self-confidence and overall well-being.

I am deeply grateful to my coach, Anna Garcia, who was pivotal in my healing journey. Your insights and support have led to profound breakthroughs that have been instrumental in my personal growth. Also to Jay Sherry for providing me with a platform to help me achieve my dreams.

Finally, I extend my heartfelt thanks to my clients, friends, and extended family. Your encouragement, accountability, and belief in my journey have been invaluable. You have helped me become more self-aware, and I am forever grateful for the role each of you has played in my life.

INTRODUCTION

I've been reading self-help books for as long as I can remember. Yet, here I am, still wondering why I keep taking these wrong turns!

It wasn't that the advice was bad. These books talked about self love, self worth, setting goals, staying positive, making smart choices, and having good communication. It all made perfect sense. They've always offered clarity, a sense of direction, and the comfort of knowing I wasn't alone in wanting to improve my life.

They pointed the way to better decisions and inspired me to try. But the truth is, there's a massive gap between reading *"Believe in yourself!"* and actually feeling that belief deep in your heart. For me, closing that gap wasn't simple or straightforward. I couldn't just wake up one day and make it happen—it took years of living through tough experiences. I made mistakes, took wrong turns, and learned many lessons the hard way. Life, with all its unpredictability and raw emotions, doesn't follow the neat formulas those books provide. No amount of motivational advice could prepare me for the storms I faced, the mistakes I made, or the gut-wrenching lessons I had to learn to truly believe in myself.

The truth is, life is anything but neat and predictable. It refuses to conform to a simple formula like "think positive, and everything will fall into place." Emotions are messy and unpredictable, often steering us onto paths we never planned to take. There's no universal solution, no one-size-fits-all approach, because we're all uniquely wired with our own struggles, fears, and dreams. Over time, I've also come to realise that there's no absolute right or wrong in life. Each of us has our own journey, our own calling, and what feels like the right path for one person may look completely different for another.

This book isn't about handing you some universal truth or a list of instructions to follow. I'm not here to tell you how to live your life. Instead, I want to share my journey—the missteps, the victories, and the hard lessons I've gathered along the way. Through these stories, you might see bits of your own life, recognise familiar mistakes, and perhaps uncover a new perspective or path forward.

Life is unpredictable. It throws us curveballs—some we barely notice, others that knock us off our feet. Yet, every challenge holds the potential to teach us something, to help us grow. It's in those moments of struggle that we can reflect, adapt, and start building a life that feels authentic and true to who we are.

So, as you turn the page, come with me on this journey. Together, let's dive into the messy, unpredictable beauty of life, and discover the strength, resilience, and courage that lie within each of us.

CONTENTS

Chapter 1

THE BEGINNING OF LIFE'S ADVENTURE

A. Echoes of Disappointment	15
B. Struggling to Fit in	16
C. The Love that Lifted Me	18
D. My Identity	18

Chapter 2

FROM PRINCESS TO WARRIOR

A. Papa's Little Princess	23
B. The Guilt of Being a Rebel	25
C. The Warrior	27

Chapter 3

SAYING 'YES' FOR THE WRONG REASONS

A. My Idea of Picture Perfect	31
B. The Societal Pressure Cooker	33
C. The Arranged Marriage Mirage	34
D. The Blurred Lines of Desperation and Desire	35

Chapter 4

BLINDED BY HOPE

A. The Waiting Game	39
B. The Dowry System's Shadow	41
C. The One-Sided Investment	42
D. The Whispers of Doubt I Ignored	43

Chapter 5

LOSING MYSELF IN MARRIAGE

A. My Quest to Be the Ideal Wife	47
B. A Wake-up Call	49
C. Resentment Rreplaced Romance	51
D. His Dream Became My Dream	53

Chapter 6

SEXUAL STIGMA AND INTIMACY

A. Sex Stigmatised	59
B. Love Languages Lost in Translation	61

Chapter 7

MOTHERHOOD

A. Pregnancy in Silence	67
B. New Beginnings, New Challenges	69
C. The Mirror Effect	71

Chapter 8

SEPARATION

A. When the Universe is Listening to You	77
B. When Hope Fights Reality	80
C. Broken Trust, Broken Heart	82
E. The Turning Point	87

Chapter 9

THE SHIFT IN BALANCE

A. The Bitter Invasion	91
B. Battling Betrayal 2 Against 1	93

Chapter 10
ALL ABOUT FINANCES

A. Financial Intelligence	97
B. The Legal Battle	99

Chapter 11
THROUGH THE PAIN, TOWARDS FORGIVENESS AND FREEDOM

A. Leaning into the Storm, Feeling the Pain	105
B. Forgiveness: The First Step to Letting Go of Victimhood	106

Chapter 12
FROM HEARTBREAK TO SELF-DISCOVERY

A. A New Purpose	111
B. Reclaiming My Identity	112
C. Embracing Solitude and Cultivating Inner Strength	115

Chapter 13
NAVIGATING LIFE WITH A NARCISSISTIC EX

A. Understanding Who I Am Dealing With	121
B. Co-Parenting with a Narcissistic Ex	122
C. Mastering the Art of Detachment and Setting Boundaries	123

Chapter 14
UNAPOLOGETICALLY ME: THE WOMAN I HAVE BECOME

Chapter 15
I CAN SEE CLEARLY NOW

A. It All Begins with You: The Most Important Relationship   131
B. Life is All About Meanings and Emotions   133
C. Life is Happening to Shape Me, Not Break Me   134
D. Pain Travels Through Generations   136
E. The Battle was Always Within   137
F. Consistency is The Key   139

Chapter 16

MASCULINE AND FEMININE ENERGIES

A. Stepping into Masculine Energy   141
B. Understanding Masculine and Feminine Energies   142
C. How Masculine Energy Eroded Our Connection   143
D. Restoring Harmony Within Myself   145

Chapter 17

DATING AFTER DIVORCE

ABOUT THE AUTHOR

Kshama Singhi's life journey is a remarkable tale of resilience, growth, and unwavering strength. Born in Mumbai, India, *Kshama* ventured to the United Kingdom, where she has lived, worked and thrived. Her path has been marked by significant challenges that have imparted profound wisdom and fuelled her passion to empower others facing similar circumstances.

From the heartbreaking experience of losing a parent at a young age to the complexities of moving countries and adapting to life as an expatriate, *Kshama* has navigated numerous transitions with grace. She has faced the hurdles of settling into a new culture, overcoming the emotional landscape of divorce, and raising a child on her own. Each of these experiences has shaped her into the compassionate and insightful Jay Shetty Certified Coach she is today.

Kshama holds no regrets about her past challenges; instead, she is deeply thankful for the lessons they have taught her and the person they have helped her become. Her dedication to helping others stems from a genuine understanding of hardship and a heartfelt desire to guide individuals toward finding strength, resilience, and fulfilment in their own lives. *Kshama Singhi* continues to inspire and uplift those on their transformative journeys through her coaching and writing.

1

THE BEGINNING OF
LIFE'S ADVENTURE

"The mind is everything. What you think you become"
– Buddha

A. ECHOES OF DISAPPOINTMENT

I was met with disappointment the day I was born. As I lay wrapped in a hospital blanket, my grandmother's disapproving words echoed: *"Ek to chhori, upar se kaali."* (In English: "As if being a girl wasn't bad enough, she's dark-skinned too").

Back then, in India, fairness was tragically equated with beauty. If you weren't fair-skinned, you were often considered unattractive—a cruel and profoundly ingrained bias. But the stigma of my birth wasn't just about skin colour. It was also because I was born a girl.

At the time, many families dreaded the arrival of daughters. The reason? The oppressive dowry system. Raising a girl meant shouldering the financial strain of her marriage, which traditionally required giving a substantial dowry—money, property, or expensive gifts—to the groom's family. From the moment a daughter was born, she was often seen as a financial burden.

While the dowry system has been legally banned and times have changed, the shadows of this tradition linger. The expectation of giving lavish gifts at weddings still hangs over many families, keeping some old biases alive.

As a child, I endured countless remedies and harsh treatments, all aimed at lightening my dark skin. My skin tone was viewed as a flaw that needed fixing. My mother, desperate to help, tried everything people suggested. Someone convinced her that unpasteurised milk would work miracles, so every weekend, she smeared it on my skin. It was smelly, sticky, and utterly disgusting. The stench was unbearable, and even today, the mere thought of drinking plain milk makes me nauseous.

From the very beginning, I felt inadequate. This sense of not being enough seeped into every part of my life, shaping my perceptions and colouring my experiences. My childhood was a maze of insecurities, each turn revealing another flaw I thought I had, another reason to believe I wasn't worthy.

These feelings didn't appear out of nowhere—they were cultivated and nurtured by the words and actions of those around me. ”*Ek to chhori, upar se kaali.*” Those words haunted me for years, embedding themselves deep into my self-identity and shaping how I saw myself and my place in the world.

B. STRUGGLING TO FIT IN

Not only was I born dark-skinned, but I also turned out to be a chubby child. In a family with three other girls, constant comparisons were common. My two cousins, who were the same age as me, were slimmer and wore clothes I could never fit into. My mom always had to buy a size bigger for me, which only added to my growing insecurity. If my skin colour made me feel unattractive, my weight made me feel outright ugly. At school, I became an easy target for bullies. Even at home, though my cousins loved me dearly, they often called me «*motu*»—a nickname that meant *fatso.* They didn't mean to hurt me, but each time they said it, it stung. What they saw as harmless affection left a lasting mark on my fragile self-esteem.

The teasing didn't stop there. Family gatherings became a dreaded ordeal. Relatives would look me up and down with judgment, making remarks disguised as concern: *"She'll never find a husband looking like that,"* as if my worth was solely tied to my appearance and the likelihood of getting married.

Snide comments like *"Don't break the chair"* or *"You look like a mom from the back"* became a regular part of my life. Each word chipped away at my already shaky confidence, reinforcing the idea that I wasn't good enough.

The emotional pain soon turned into physical avoidance. I began to hate mirrors and avoided them whenever I could. I wore baggy clothes, hoping to hide my body and disappear into the background. When it came to my looks, all I wanted was to be invisible.

Ironically, food became both my comfort and my enemy. I would binge in secret, using food to numb the pain, only to be consumed by guilt and shame afterwards. It became a vicious cycle—one I couldn't seem to break. Compliments, when they came, felt insincere, and I dismissed them as pity.

At home, things weren't much better. My parents, desperate to help, enforced strict diets on me and my sister, while they let my cousins eat whatever they wanted. They removed essentials like ghee and rice from my meals, unaware of the long-term harm it would cause. I didn't just suffer from nutritional deprivation—I felt emotionally starved, too.

Desperation pushed me to try every fad diet I found. I counted calories, starved myself, and followed extreme regimes. The numbers on the scale dropped for a short time, but the results never lasted. Every time I felt low, I binged, and the weight always returned, leaving me more defeated than before.

My parents even forced me to go to the gym, though I had no interest in it. It felt more like punishment than a step toward health. While my cousins lived carefree, I faced constant reminders of everything I couldn't eat or do.

My struggle with my body and self-image overshadowed every part of my life. I wasn't just fighting my weight—I was fighting myself. Shame, insecurity, and hopelessness trapped me in a cycle I couldn't escape. For years, I couldn't imagine a future where my weight or skin colour didn't define me. The battle felt exhausting, relentless, and all-consuming.

C. THE LOVE THAT LIFTED ME

My childhood wasn't just about struggles and insecurities—it overflowed with joy and love. Even when I doubted my looks, I still found countless reasons to smile and embrace life. My cheerful nature, bright smile, and carefree spirit won over my family and extended relatives. I made friends easily, and to my delight, many male family members showed me a special fondness, even more than my cousins. Being surrounded by so much love and positivity felt terrific.

I was a happy-go-lucky girl who lived fearlessly. I did what I wanted without worrying about being scolded by my parents. I was bold and authentic, often managing to get my way with the grown-ups when my cousins couldn't.

Three pillars in my life—my grandfather, papa, and uncle—nurtured this sense of freedom and confidence. Their unwavering belief in me became my sanctuary, something I clung to when the world seemed determined to remind me of my flaws. They saw potential in me when I couldn't see it in myself. Their love and encouragement became my lifeline, helping me build resilience in the face of self-doubt.

I vividly remember my grandfather's loving words, how my papa's eyes lit up with pride at even my smallest achievements, and how my uncle made no secret that I was his favourite. Among all the children in the family, I was the one who could get away with anything and the only one who could convince these strong-headed men to see things my way. These moments felt like treasures, tiny but powerful reminders that I mattered, was capable, and deserving of love. They made me feel strong, even in the face of my insecurities. I believed I could achieve anything I set my mind to—so long as it had nothing to do with my looks.

D. MY IDENTITY

It's no surprise that my identity became solidified as *"the dark, chubby girl"*. This wasn't just a harmless label—it became the lens through which I saw myself. And that lens was distorted, tinted with self-loathing and insecurity.

The label itself wasn't the real issue, but the meaning I attached to it tore me apart. To me, *"dark, chubby girl"* didn't just describe my appearance—it meant „*UGLY.*" That's who I believed I was at my core: just *UGLY.*

Yet, ironically, I was also the *"dark, chubby girl"* who was strong and loveable. Deep down, I knew my family cherished me. Their affection and support gave me glimpses of my worth, but it came with a shadow of doubt. I couldn't help but believe that their love was an exception. I convinced myself that no one outside my family could see past my looks or find me deserving of their love.

This self-perception didn't remain a passing thought—it seeped into my identity, growing into a deeply rooted belief that it shaped every aspect of my life. It told me I was unworthy of being seen, heard, or valued. It became the biggest roadblock in my journey, keeping me small and invisible.

This belief prevented me from stepping out of my comfort zone or embracing new experiences. Opportunities that could have helped me grow were ignored or rejected.

My feelings of inadequacy overshadowed even simple joys like learning to ride a bike or playing a game of tennis. I carried the weight of my insecurities into social interactions, constantly feeling judged and scrutinised.

But the most damaging effect of all was the erosion of my self-love. Looking in the mirror, I couldn't see anything good or beautiful. My mind was fixated on my perceived flaws, leaving no room to appreciate my strengths, talents, or the unique person I was.

The label of dark, chubby girl overshadowed the identity of being strong and loveable. Over time, the *substantial, dark, chubby* parts of me remained, but somewhere along the way, I lost the loveable parts of me. This loss stifled my growth, crushed my dreams, and blinded me to the possibilities of who I could become.

It was a heavy burden to carry, one that weighed not only on my body but also on my spirit. Despite knowing my family loved me, I couldn't shake the feeling that the world beyond them saw me as unworthy

WORNG TURN, RIGHT LESSONS

and unlovable. This paradox left me in a painful cycle—yearning for validation yet unable to believe I deserved it.

WHAT I KNOW NOW

1. WE ALL BATTLE IN DIFFERENT WAYS: Growing up, we all collect beliefs about ourselves—both good and bad. This is simply part of life. No matter how loving or flawed your family is, no matter how nurturing or challenging your environment, it's inevitable that we form beliefs as we navigate the world.

Some of these beliefs empower us, while others limit us. Yet, humans tend to focus on the negative ones, often exaggerating their importance. These limiting beliefs can feel overwhelming, and it doesn't take much—a word, a look, or a situation—to trigger them. This isn't anyone's fault; it's just a part of being human.

A recent conversation with one of the cousins I grew up with gave me a fresh perspective on this. She shared how, as a child, she often felt unimportant because everyone in the family listened to me over anybody else. While I obsessed over my appearance and felt inadequate, she battled her insecurities, feeling overlooked and left out because I received more attention.

This conversation opened my eyes to the irony of our experiences. While I felt ugly and unworthy in comparison to them, they felt unloved and unseen in contrast to me. It was a profound reminder of how personal and unique individual experiences and perceptions shape insecurities.

Looking back, it's clear that everyone is carrying their own burdens, no matter how perfect their lives might seem from the outside. Our beliefs—especially the limiting ones—may shape our perspectives, but they don't have to define who we are. Recognising this truth is the first step toward breaking free from their hold.

2. THE POWER OF BELIEF:
Mahatma Gandhi once said:
"Your beliefs become your thoughts,

Your thoughts become your words,
Your words become your actions,
Your actions become your habits,
Your habits become your values,
Your values become your destiny."
This timeless wisdom captures a powerful truth: we don't manifest what we wish for—we manifest what we truly believe in. My beliefs and inner narrative held me back from living authentically for years. I missed out on exciting opportunities and meaningful connections because I allowed my doubts and fears to control me.

Now, I understand that I have the power to change this. My beliefs aren't fixed—they can evolve. I see myself as the author of my own life. By rewriting my beliefs, I reshape my story and open the door to possibilities I once thought were out of reach.

As you read through the following chapters, you'll see how my beliefs shaped my life and led me to take wrong turns. But you'll also see something else—how that same person, armed with the courage to challenge and change her belief system, transformed her life into something she once thought impossible. My journey proves that change is possible, no matter how deeply ingrained those beliefs may seem. Don't get me wrong—it's not that I don't fall back sometimes or that my old identity doesn't try to creep in. It does, often. But the difference now is that my new belief system comes rushing in alongside it, bringing proof of how my thinking is shaping my life. It gives me a choice: to remain a victim of my old, limiting beliefs or to embrace new, empowering ones. And every time I choose empowerment, I reclaim a little more of my life.

3. CONFIDENCE IS THE REAL BEAUTY: Beauty has no definition—it's about embracing and accepting yourself for who you are. When you accept yourself, you exude confidence, which becomes your beauty. It's like silently announcing to the world, *"I am beautiful, and you should think so too."*

Self-acceptance creates a ripple effect: when you embrace yourself, others also accept you. This acceptance silences the voice of self-doubt, replacing it with empowerment. In my journey, as I started to see myself for who I was and embraced my unique self, something remarkable happened. I began receiving more compliments as if the nagging remarks and criticisms of the past had vanished.

It became clear that how I saw myself directly influenced how others saw me. I gave the same light to the world by seeing myself in a new light. This is who I am, and I now expect the world to see me no differently. True beauty starts with how you see and value yourself.

2

FROM PRINCESS TO WARRIOR

*"When someone you love becomes a memory,
the memory becomes a treasure"*

- Unknown

A. PAPA'S LITTLE PRINCESS

Like any other family, ours was a mix of joy and conflict. While there was endless love and laughter, there were also quarrels and disagreements. The arguments were just as frequent as the hugs, whether over toys, shared responsibilities, or simply stepping on each other's toes in our crowded household

The two shared everything, from recipes and chores to their worries and joys. But living so closely also meant the occasional flare-ups—arguments over minor things or even moments of jealousy that would bubble to the surface.

My Papa was a simple, hard-working man. Kind and intelligent, he devoured books like a scholar and ran multiple businesses with strength and determination. His booming voice could make the whole house jump, yet I never doubted his love. I often teased him by calling him "puppy" instead of Papa, a nickname he didn't particularly like. He would scold me gently, shaking his head in mock disapproval, but it was never serious. He rarely got truly angry with me—so infrequently that I can count those moments on one hand.

One crisp Saturday in October, the house buzzed with energy. My sister was hosting a party, and Papa had promised to come home early from work to help. While my sister prepared for her crowd of older friends, I had no interest in joining them. At 14, I was content watching TV with my cousin, our laughter mingling with the sounds of the bustling house.

Then, the phone rang. The mood shifted instantly. My uncle answered, his voice cheerful, but as the conversation unfolded, his face turned pale, his laughter replaced by something I couldn't quite name. He hung up, trembling, and hurried outside, muttering about the hospital.

The party's excitement evaporated, leaving a suffocating silence. My stomach churned as unease began to creep in. Something was wrong—wrong—with Papa. My older sister dropped everything to pray, her words tumbling out in whispers that carried a desperate urgency. My aunt made frantic calls, her voice a mix of panic and disbelief.

And then, the second call came, shattering whatever hope remained.

Papa was gone, just like that. A heart attack had stolen him away in the blink of an eye. No warnings, no goodbyes—he had ceased to be.

How was that even possible? I couldn't believe it. People don't just vanish like that, do they? Don't they fall sick first, giving you time to prepare? He'd been fine that morning, his usual self. It felt impossible—like some cruel mistake. My Papa couldn't be gone. Not him.

As the news spread, the house filled with the sound of grief. My mother's sobs pierced the air, her heartbreak mirrored by the wails of relatives who had rushed to our side. It was chaos, a storm of sorrow that swept through our home.

Early the following day, they brought him home from the hospital. He lay in the middle of the living room, his body limp and still. I peeked out from one of the rooms, wanting nothing more than to run into his arms and beg him to wake up. But I couldn't gather the courage to go near his lifeless form.

Our house became a whirlwind of activity as they prepared for the funeral. Relatives and friends arrived in a blur of tearful embraces. Mom was a statue of grief, consumed by her pain. My heart ached, but tears refused to come. Perhaps it was too much, too fast to process. I felt adrift; my world turned upside down. No more jokes with "puppy."

The days that followed were a blur of condolences, whispered secrets, and the sounds of sobs and tears hanging in the air.

Life as I knew it had shattered.

In a single day, my life had turned upside down. I was no longer someone's little princess, shielded from the world's harshness. In one unthinkable moment, Uncertainty engulfed me, with waves threatening to pull me under. I spent years—decades—learning how to swim again.

B. THE GUILT OF BEING A REBEL

Life was never the same after my papa's passing. His absence left a vacuum in our lives that nothing could fill.

As the dust of reality settled, I clung to normalcy. I went to school on autopilot and met with overwhelming sympathy from those around me. Relatives, though well-meaning, often made things worse. They never missed an opportunity to discuss the tragedy, making every visit a reminder of how pitiful our situation had become. Their words cut deeper than they realised, and I often wished my mom would stop meeting them altogether.

Our home became a space heavy with sadness, an unspoken grief that hung in the air for years. The foundation of our family had crumbled, leaving us vulnerable and unsure of what lay ahead. My mom, once a symbol of quiet strength, now bore the weight of unimaginable loss. She was drowning in grief, raising three children, struggling with finances she had no experience managing and navigating a strained relationship with my uncle.

As the weeks turned into months and years, life continued, but not without hardship. My sister, driven by necessity, found a job earlier than planned, stepping into responsibilities far beyond her years. I finished school and, with a flicker of hope, secured a place at one of the best colleges in town.

At college, my three groups of friends became my lifeline. Each played an important role in helping me navigate the new chapters of my life. My girls were my anchor, the family I created outside my home, where I felt safe and understood. The two boys I befriended brought a different kind of companionship. Initially, I felt like the third wheel in their friendship, but their company grew on me over time. One became the brother I chose, while the other—the one I had a secret crush on—later became my closest confidant and best friend. Then there was my third group, the adventurous, carefree crew, who opened doors to a vibrant world of experiences I'd never imagined. With them, I ventured out, tried new things, and momentarily forgot the chaos waiting for me back home.

Life began to feel a little less bleak, a little more hopeful.

But no amount of friendship could completely shield me from the growing cracks in my family's fragile reality. While I was busy building my life in college, the weight of grief and financial strain bore heavily on my mom. The tension between her and my uncle, which had been simmering for years, began to boil over. Each interaction deepened the rift, and the house that had once felt like a sanctuary now echoed with unspoken resentments and visible divides.

Her desperation to find some semblance of stability led her to a painful decision: she would leave Mumbai, our home, and move to a small town called Indore, where her second brother lived. She hoped the move would give her emotional support and a fresh start.

But this meant leaving everything I knew—my city, college, and friends. As a teenager, the idea of giving up everything and moving in with my mom ignited a fiery rebellion within me. I felt hope and progress slipping away. I saw only a bleak future filled with regret and resentment.

"It's not fair!" I cried out in frustration. "Why should I have to sacrifice everything? My sister is past her teens and has a career, and my brother is too young to understand. Why is it on me?" My mom's needs and pain blurred in the haze of my self-preservation.

"You never support me!" she said, her voice heavy with hurt. She repeated those words so often that they became my new reality, a constant reminder of my supposed selfishness and failure as a daughter.

But I couldn't let go of my decision. I dug in my heels, insisting on staying in Mumbai to complete my education. The guilt, however, began to grow, quietly settling into my subconscious.

The fight lasted for months, a battle of wills between my mom and me. Ultimately, she gave in, but her resentment lingered for long after. My family moved to Indore—my mom, sister, and brother—while I stayed behind in Mumbai, creating not just a physical distance but an emotional one.

Despite the pain of our separation, there was one silver lining: my mom found the support she sought in her brother and sister-in-law in Indore. But for me, the guilt of my rebellion stayed a quiet shadow that followed me through the years.

C. THE WARRIOR

Winning the battle to stay in Mumbai felt like a victory, but it was just the beginning of a much more brutal fight.

My mom, grappling with her financial struggles, reluctantly told me she couldn't afford to support me while I stayed behind. She agreed to send me ₹3000 a month (about £30) to cover all my living expenses. Still, it came with a condition: I couldn't continue living in the family home. The tension between her and my uncle had reached a point where she worried his family might influence me if I stayed. She told me to find a place to rent.

At the time, I felt like my mom made every decision to push me toward giving up and joining her in Indore. She offered me only ₹3000, which wasn't enough to rent a room, let alone cover other expenses. I searched for affordable accommodation near my university for weeks, but the task felt impossible. I was adrift, caught in a storm of grief, loneliness, and growing resentment. My friends became my lifeline, offering support when I needed it most, but inside, I was battling guilt and doubt.

I felt guilty for not being a better daughter, not supporting my mom in her time of need, and choosing my independence over my family's unity. I sometimes questioned my decision and thought about giving in to her demands. But each time I imagined myself in Indore, dependent on relatives and far from everything I knew, it made me shudder.

The thought of losing my independence strengthened my resolve. I was determined to carve out a life for myself, no matter how difficult.

Desperation drove me to fight harder. I pleaded with my mom to let me stay in the family home. After many heated arguments, she reluctantly agreed, but under strict conditions: I couldn't accept any favours from my uncle or aunt, I had to cook my own meals, pay my own bills, and limit my interactions with them. Though it felt like I was walking a tightrope, I agreed without hesitation.

To make ends meet, I needed a job. Determined to take control of my life, I found work as a web designer, securing full-time employment even before I turned 18. My days became a whirlwind—I attended college in the mornings, worked after classes, and spent evenings and weekends with friends who had become my chosen family.

There were days when the weight felt unbearable, and I wanted to give up. But each setback only fuelled my determination. I learned to navigate through the pain and turn it into strength.

Without my friends and cousins, Mumbai—my birthplace—might have felt unfamiliar and isolating. They were the thread that kept me tied to a sense of belonging amidst the chaos. My girl group became my second family, showing up almost every weekend, uninvited but always welcome, filling the empty spaces of my life with laughter and companionship. When I felt overwhelmed or low, my best friend would show up without fail, sitting with me for hours, offering comfort with her words and unwavering presence. Another friend, with a kindness that touched my heart, often brought me home-cooked meals, leaving them at my place before I even returned from work. They didn't just support me; they helped me rediscover the warmth and connection I desperately needed during those turbulent times.

On the other hand, my confidence in my career started to grow. As I worked harder, I achieved success and gained credibility at my workplace. Within a few months, I was earning enough to support myself, no longer needing to ask my mom for money. I had taken control of my life in a way I hadn't imagined possible. Without even realising it, I was turning my pain into my power. Though the journey was incredibly difficult, it was one of immense growth. I was learning, evolving, and finding strength I never knew I had, not just in my career but as a human being.

I started to feel that I had learned to survive on my own. My identity was shifting—I was no longer just the girl who had to rely on others. I had become strong and independent, someone who could do whatever she wanted. That newfound confidence was becoming an inseparable part of who I was. The struggle, the pain, and the loneliness had all shaped me into a person who could face the world head-on, knowing that no matter what, I would always find a way to rise.

WHAT I KNOW NOW

1. **LIFE IS CO-CREATION:** One of the most powerful realisations I've encountered is that life is a co-creation. We often think everything that happens to us is out of our control. Still, as I reflect on my journey, I can see how much of it was spiritually co-created by the people in my life, especially my papa and my mom. We were all playing a part in shaping my journey and the lessons I came into this world for, even if we didn't fully understand it then.

I co-created my world with my papa for most of my early years. He was my protector, my provider, the one I looked up to for guidance. I felt safe, shielded, and loved. But when he passed away unexpectedly, I found myself facing the world without the safety net I had always known. His death left me vulnerable, unshielded, and without the protection I had always relied on. At first, I resented him for leaving so early. I wondered why he couldn't stay or shield me from the harshness of life. It felt unfair, and I struggled with that loss for a long time.

However, as time passed, I began to understand that his passing, though painful, was a pivotal moment in my journey. Strangely, I realised now that it was exactly what I needed. While my papa was around, I lived in a bubble, cocooned in my comfort zone, with no real reason to step out or challenge myself. I was like a princess, protected by my Papa's presence but limited by it. Only after he left did life push me into the deep end, forcing me to learn how to swim on my own. His absence became the catalyst for my growth, independence, and strength.

Looking back, I can see that everything, even the painful moments, was necessary to become who I am today. I co-created my life with my papa and mom, but their contributions were part of a bigger plan I couldn't yet see. Their love, choices, presence, and absence all shaped me and prepared me for the challenges ahead. Life, I've come to understand, is never a solitary journey. We are all co-creating our stories, often without even realising it.

2. THE ONLY WAY TO GET THROUGH CHALLENGING TIMES IS TO FOCUS ON THE NEXT BEST STEP: When everything feels like falling apart, it's easy to get overwhelmed. At that point, thinking about the big picture can feel like trying to climb a mountain that's too high to reach. There were many times when I felt like I couldn't go on, and the weight of my circumstances felt unbearable. I often wanted to escape everything because the future seemed uncertain and complex.

But then I realised that the only way to survive difficult times is to break them down into small, manageable pieces. Instead of stressing over what would happen next year or in five years, I learned to focus on the next best step I could take right at that moment. It could be something small—like applying for a job, getting through a day at work, or even calling a friend for support. Each little step made a difference, and slowly, those steps began to add up.

For example, when I decided to stay in Mumbai, I was overwhelmed by the thought of living alone, managing everything alone, and the pressure of financially supporting myself. But I couldn't think about the future all at once, so I focused on the next thing—finding a place to live. Then, once I had a place, I focused on getting a job, one thing at a time. And each small step gave me the strength to keep moving forward. It wasn't easy, but I could build the foundation I needed to keep going by focusing on what I could do right then instead of trying to solve everything at once.

3

SAYING 'YES' FOR THE WRONG REASONS

"I am not a product of my circumstances.
I am a product of my decisions."

– Stephen Covey

A. MY IDEA OF PICTURE PERFECT

I think we can all agree that there's something about a good rom-com that pulls you in. The meet-cutes, the grand gestures, the happily-ever-afters—they paint such a perfect picture of love that it almost feels like it's too good to resist. I remember watching movies like *The Proposal*, where Ryan Reynolds is the charming, successful guy ready to sweep you off your feet in the most extravagant way. Or *How to Lose a Guy in 10 Days*, with Matthew McConaughey's character who goes to any length to win over Kate Hudson's heart. And, of course, there's Shahrukh Khan in *Dilwale Dulhania Le Jayenge*, whose love for Kajol is so deep it's practically magical.

My young heart was obsessed with these stories, and My idea of "picture-perfect" love was shaped by these Hollywood and Bollywood fantasies.

These characters set the bar impossibly high. They made me believe that true love meant grand, over-the-top gestures, with knights in shining armour swooping in to solve all my problems. They sold me the fantasy that love was fated, a magical connection that swept you off your feet. But what those movies never showed was the everyday reality—the struggles, the compromises, and the effort it takes to build a lasting relationship. They made love look effortless, as if destiny would handle everything.

And yet, there I was, caught in the pull of this idealised version of love. I was still that girl— the one struggling with insecurities. I wasn't the confident, carefree person I wanted to be. The reality of my appearance, the old identity of being the chubby, dark-skinned girl, weighed heavily on me. I secretly hoped for my knight in shining armour to come, rescue me from my struggles, and transform my self-image by making me feel beautiful—to rebuild the protective shield I'd lost when my papa passed away.

But despite my deep insecurities, I couldn't see the boys around me who genuinely wanted to get to know me. I brushed off their compliments, ignored their attempts to connect, and even dragged my cousin along when I now realised they were probably asking me out. I was so caught up in the idea of finding something perfect that I couldn't recognise what was right in front of me.

Then there were the boys I liked and had a crush on. For brief moments, I'd muster the Then there were the boys I liked, the ones I had crushes on. For brief moments, I would summon the courage to put myself out there, dropping hints about how I felt. But every time, I was met with rejection. The hardest blow came from my best friend—the boy I had secretly liked for months. He turned me down, and it felt like my heart shattered in an instant. At that point in my life, when I was already struggling with conflict at home with my mom, his rejection felt like the last straw. Although we can laugh and joke about it now, at the time, it stung deeply, pushing me further into a place of hurt and self-doubt. I felt like my worst fear had been confirmed—I was not good enough. I was unworthy of the love that I had seen in the movies, the kind I had dreamed of for so long. Although he turned me down, he didn't abandon me. He continued to be my friend, always there to talk for hours when I was feeling low, offering a listening ear and comfort when I needed it most.

The thoughts swirled in my head, and I started to believe them. That voice in my head—my inner critic—had a field day. It told me I was ugly and unlovable and that no one would ever want me the way I wanted to be wanted. That maybe real love, the kind that I had dreamed about, just wasn't meant for me.

B. THE SOCIETAL PRESSURE COOKER

After two painful rejections and the constant whispers of my inner critic, I convinced myself that love just wasn't meant for me. I had already given up on the idea of finding someone who would see me for who I truly was.

But the pressure from society didn't disappear—it only grew louder. In my culture, marriage is considered a fundamental part of life. The message was clear: "Find a husband, settle down, that's what you're supposed to do." As I reached my mid-20s, the questions began to pile up: "Why aren't you married yet?" "Don't you want children?" Society painted a picture of the perfect timeline—graduate from college, get a job, meet your husband, marry by 24, and have kids by 28. Anyone who didn't follow this so-called "ideal" path was seen as somehow failing at life.

It felt like a ticking time bomb was fast approaching, and if I didn't find someone soon, it would explode. Every passing year seemed like a step closer to being left behind. The pressure made my confidence crack a little more each day as I questioned if I would ever fit into this perfect mould everyone expected me to.

At the same time, I was doing well in my career, excelling at work and gaining recognition. But it seemed irrelevant. No one asked about my achievements or celebrated my success. The focus was always on what was missing. No one noticed my growth or the strength I was building in other areas of my life. Instead, the spotlight was always on the lack of a partner, the absence of marriage, and the ticking clock that made me feel like I was running out of time.

Under this weight of expectation, my belief that I was unlovable only grew stronger. The fear of missing out—watching everyone else live the life I thought I should be living—began to haunt me. I started to wonder if maybe I was the one who was wrong, the one being left behind while everyone else followed the script.

C. THE ARRANGED MARRIAGE MIRAGE

The idea of an arranged marriage felt like a lifeline. In my culture, arranged marriages have been a long-standing tradition, where families take the responsibility of finding a suitable match. There was a sense of comfort in thinking that my family, with their wisdom and love, would find someone who was compatible with me. If things didn't work out, it felt less like a personal failure and more like a shared responsibility—something that we could all face together.

However, over time, this tradition evolved into something much less personal. It became more about ticking boxes—an impersonal checklist that ignored real emotions and individual desires. The less confident I felt about myself, the fewer boxes I checked. And so, when my mother asked if I was seeing anyone and offered to help find a match, I willingly handed over the responsibility to her and my family, hoping they could find someone who could fill the void I felt in my life.

My cousin took it a step further and began his own search for a match. He introduced me to a boy who lived in the UK with his family, who was still in India. I had already given up on the idea of finding love for myself, so I agreed to the proposal. But, to my surprise, his family wasn't as enthusiastic. Despite his father's disapproval, we proceeded with the engagement. Looking back, I often wonder what I was thinking at the time.

From the start, there was no real attraction between us. We shared a few moments together, but it quickly became clear that our relationship was filled with complications. The distance, the cultural differences, and the lack of genuine connection made it feel like a mismatch from the beginning. My family, recognising this, suggested I call off the engagement, and without much hesitation, I did.

Ending the engagement was incredibly difficult. It wasn't that I missed him—there was no deep emotional connection—but I feared the judgment and whispers from society. People constantly asked why it ended, and all I could offer was a vague explanation. The real pain wasn't from losing the relationship but from the stigma of being the one to break it off. My mother, stressed and overwhelmed, seemed almost relieved to send me back to Mumbai for my job, perhaps hoping that time and distance would give me some clarity.

The entire experience left me feeling more isolated and disheartened than ever before. What was supposed to be a solution had only added to the weight of my insecurities. It wasn't just about a broken engagement—it was about the fear of not being good enough for anyone and the constant pressure to conform to expectations that never quite fit who I was.

D. THE BLURRED LINES OF DESPERATION AND DESIRE

You'd think by now I would have learned my lesson, but I hadn't. In fact, I was a little slow—okay, very slow. The weight of the broken engagement, societal pressure, and the constant ticking clock felt suffocating. With everything weighing on me, I was heading straight into desperation.

Despite the turmoil, a part of me still yearned for love—a deep, real connection with someone who would see me for who I was. But my inner critic didn't make it easy. It whispered cruel things: "You're not good enough," "Just say yes to whoever is willing," "Beggars can't be choosers," "As long as he's not overweight, just accept it," "You won't find anyone else", "You're ugly and unworthy," and "You're not getting any younger." The fear of being alone was louder than anything else.

So, when another marriage proposal came along, it seemed like my only option. The "suitable boy" my family had found agreed to marry me, and in a moment of sheer desperation, I said yes.

I felt tiny butterflies, little flutters of excitement and hope—maybe, just maybe, love was on the horizon. But more than that, I felt relief. It felt like an escape from the judgment, not only from others but from myself. Perhaps now, I could finally convince myself that I was pretty, lovable, and worthy of someone's attention.

As news of the engagement spread, my cousins and friends started pointing out the obvious—we didn't look compatible. They commented on how I had a better career, lifestyle, and future than him. And yet, I ignored them all.

Deep down, a small voice warned me. It told me that this relationship wasn't right for me. But that voice was drowned out by my insecurities and the overwhelming roar of fear and doubt. Instead of listening to my heart, I gave in to the pressure of my fears and society's expectations, making a decision that would change the course of my life forever.

WHAT I KNOW NOW

1. IT'S NOT REJECTION, IT'S RE-DIRECTION: At the time, rejection feels like a blow to your self-worth. It stings, it makes you question everything, and you wonder if you'll ever find someone who will truly see you. But, looking back now, I realise that rejection was not the end—it was just life pointing me in a different direction. For example, when my best friend rejected me, I was devastated. I thought I had lost my chance at love. But now, I can see that his rejection was a blessing in disguise. We were not right for each other. Our values, lifestyles, and goals were poles apart. He and I would have never been able to build a lasting future together. At that time, I couldn't see it, but now I understand that life was steering me away from something that would not have been healthy or fulfilling for me. His rejection was just life clearing the way for something better.

2. LIFE PUTS YOU IN SIMILAR SITUATIONS AGAIN AND AGAIN UNTIL YOU LEARN YOUR LESSON: There's a saying that the universe will give you the same test repeatedly until you finally pass it. Reflecting on the relationships I've attracted into my life, I see this pattern so clearly now. Both times, I found myself drawn to narcissistic men, and it wasn't a coincidence—it was a reflection of my own low self-worth. The universe was sending me these experiences to teach me a crucial lesson: to recognise and embrace my own value.

The first time I got engaged, I was in a fragile and vulnerable place. I was still reeling from the pain of not having my papa around and feeling disconnected from my mom, which left me emotionally adrift. Hurt and insecure, I craved validation and comfort, desperately seeking someone to fill the void. In that state, I wasn't thinking clearly or valuing myself; I agreed to the engagement simply because I didn't want to feel alone anymore. My insecurities blinded me to what I truly deserved, and I settled for what felt like the only option at the time.

Then came my engagement to my now ex-husband, a decision shaped even more by my deep-seated belief that I wasn't worthy of love. At that point, my self-worth was at its lowest, rooted in the idea that I didn't deserve love because I didn't look good enough. This belief consumed me, making me feel like I had no choice but to accept what was offered. I convinced myself I could make it work, even as red flags became impossible to ignore and my gut instincts warned me something was terribly wrong.

In both relationships, I was the stronger, more capable person, yet I refused to see it. I buried my potential and ignored my value, convincing myself that this was all life had to offer. I settled, not because I wanted to, but because I didn't believe I deserved anything better.

The universe kept sending me signs, trying to teach me a lesson: I was worthy of so much more. But I wasn't ready to listen. Instead, I repeatedly chose people and situations that reflected my own inner struggles, trapped in a cycle until I finally broke free. It was only when I began to embrace my self-worth and see my true value that I could step out of the loop and rewrite my story for the better.

3. THE CLOCK ISN'T TICKING, AND LIFE IS NOT A FAIRY TALE: Believing in and following society's definition of success and its timeline may work for some, but it doesn't fit everyone's journey. We've all grown up watching fairy tales where love is effortless, and relationships are magically perfect. But real life is far from a 2-hour film, and relationships aren't something that just happens—they require effort, understanding, and growth. In addition, the pressure to meet society's expectations—get married by a certain age, settle down, and start a family—can feel overwhelming, but the truth is, there's no universal timeline for everyone.

For me, I constantly felt like I was behind. After two rejections, one broken engagement, and one failed marriage, I realised that I was rushing into relationships for the wrong reasons—mainly because I let society make me feel like I was running out of time and I was not worthy of love. I kept pushing myself into situations that weren't right for me simply because I thought that was what I was supposed to do. I wasn't in a place to truly understand my own needs, values, or desires. I was blindly following what society said was "correct." It wasn't until I took a step back, spent time alone, and got to know myself better that I began to understand the importance of timing—not just based on age, but based on personal growth.

To truly be in a healthy relationship, you need to first know yourself: your values, your desires, and your boundaries. Only when you're clear about who you are and what you want can you build a relationship that is meaningful, fulfilling, and right for you. The clock isn't ticking. Life is unfolding on its own terms, and it's okay to take the time you need to figure it out.

4

BLINDED BY HOPE

"Hope is a waking dream."

- Aristotle.

A. THE WAITING GAME

So, there I was—engaged to be married, and I was brimming with excitement and hope for the first time in what felt like forever. Despite all my past self-doubts, someone had chosen me and seen me as deserving of love and a lifelong commitment. For those first few days, I floated on a euphoric cloud, filled with the exhilarating thought that my dream of a fulfilling relationship had finally come true. I was someone's priority, and that realisation brought overwhelming joy and belonging.

Every moment felt magical; my heart fluttered excitedly, and my days wrapped in a dreamlike haze. We spent time together, laughing, exploring, and sharing stolen glances that made me feel special. His attention and affection felt like rays of sunlight, warming parts of me that had long been cold. It was intoxicating—the way his small gestures made me feel not just loved but cherished.

I allowed myself to lean into the joy, believing this was my "happily ever after." Everything seemed perfect. I felt like I had finally found the love I had been waiting for, and for once, I let myself enjoy the beauty of the moment, believing wholeheartedly in the story I wanted so much to be true.

Then, reality hit me like a ton of bricks. After ten magical days together, he returned to the UK, leaving an impossible void to ignore. The fairytale I had built began to feel fragile. Our time together had been a whirlwind of emotions, but now, with him thousands of miles away and planning to return only right before our wedding, excitement faded into an unsettling quiet.

Indian weddings are nothing short of a grand spectacle—a full-blown drama bursting with excitement, chaos, and high emotions. They are a whirlwind of vibrant celebrations, filled with countless traditions, endless music, colourful attire, and unavoidable clashes and arguments. With so many people involved, each carrying their expectations and opinions, the pressure to keep everyone happy is immense. Yet, amidst all the chaos, an undeniable magic makes it all worth it—at least in most cases.

Needless to say, I got very busy with the drama of wedding preparations, trying to manage family expectations, and juggling a million details that came with the excitement of an Indian wedding. But despite the whirlwind, the nine months that followed were agonising. Our long-distance relationship became a constant source of anxiety. I spent countless hours hoping the time zones would align, wishing he'd carve out a moment from his busy schedule to talk. The phone became my lifeline, but no call, no message, no words could ever replace the warmth of his presence. My heart grew heavier each day, aching for any gesture reassuring me he felt the same way I did. I longed to feel cherished during this courtship, but those moments were becoming rare. And as the distance stretched on, the red flags I had once ignored began to creep back into my thoughts, no longer easy to dismiss.

Our conversations, once filled with excitement and anticipation, started to shift. They became less about us and more about wedding logistics and family drama. The magic faded. The romance I had once dreamed of became overshadowed by the stress of navigating two families that clashed at every turn.

I silently hoped he would step up, help take some of the wedding burden off my shoulders, and manage the family conflicts. But each time, he offered the excuse of being far away. And each time, I let him off the hook, convincing myself that it wasn't fair to expect too much from him given the distance.

I had already started falling into the "perfect wife" role, lowering my expectations for grand gestures or emotional support. I knew his finances were tight and told myself not to expect more. I was teaching him how to treat me!

The happy memories of those magical ten days we spent together were fading fast, overshadowed by the overwhelming stress of wedding preparations and the tension of managing two feuding families. What had once felt like the start of a fairytale now felt like a heavy burden, and the love I had longed for seemed to be slipping further out of reach. Still, I kept making excuses for him, telling myself that everything would change once we were finally together again.

B. THE DOWRY SYSTEM'S SHADOW

India has rich traditions, but some customs linger, such as unwanted shadows. Despite being officially banned, the dowry system still casts a long, unseen presence. It's no longer just about expensive gifts; it's become a subtle power dynamic, often masked as a wedding tradition.

While most families don't openly call it a "dowry" anymore, the expectations remain unchanged. The groom's family often carries a sense of entitlement, expecting a constant flow of gifts from the bride's side. This cycle, especially in arranged marriages, begins with a conversation about the "budget"—a term used to subtly define what the bride's family will offer the groom's side.

In my case, my ex's family agreed to the wedding, but with strings attached. They expected my mother to be a perpetual giver, always ready to meet their demands. This sparked constant battles over traditions, money, and gifts, turning the wedding preparations into a battleground where both families clashed, and I got caught in the middle. I fully supported my mom's refusal to yield to their demands, but I also found myself torn, trying to keep the peace between both sides. I constantly argued with my family to maintain balance while nagging him to help resolve the situation. Yet, he rarely took a stand, using distance and time zones as excuses.

I was fighting a two-front war, and I was fighting it alone.

Despite my best efforts, I felt like I was failing miserably. The rift between me and my family only widened, with my mom and I being at odds more than ever, while his family never fully accepted me. I became the scapegoat for everyone's frustrations. No matter how hard I tried, I felt like I didn't belong anywhere.

C. THE ONE-SIDED INVESTMENT

Another red flag, a constant thorn in my side, was the total imbalance in how much my family and I were giving to the relationship. Investment isn't just about money; it's about time, energy, and emotions—everything we poured into building a future together.

My family went all in. They showered him and his family with generous gifts, their hearts full of excitement about the wedding. They saw him as part of the family, someone they wanted to welcome openly. But from him or his family, there was nothing—silence.

When we got engaged, I knew he wasn't financially well-off, so I didn't expect much financially. But I did hope for investment in other ways, like time and effort.

But when I would go out with my in-laws, they expected me to pay for everything. On my birthday, the best I got was a bouquet and a box of chocolates. It felt like a weak attempt at a gesture, but I convinced myself it was okay, thinking his lack of money excused his lack of effort. Here's the painful truth: I wasn't getting gifts because of his finances, quality time, or physical support because of the distance. I didn't feel important because I was caught in between family conflicts.

I wasn't even getting his virtual time because of his demanding job. Where, then, was his investment in me?

The lack of effort screamed disinterest, but I chose to ignore it, caught up in my beliefs and the excitement of the wedding.

D. THE WHISPERS OF DOUBT I IGNORED

There were whispers of doubt in the quiet corners of my mind, tiny voices trying to warn me of the dangers ahead. But I shoved them down, drowning them out with the noise of wedding bells. The excitement of planning, the pressure to conform, and the fear of another broken engagement all contributed to silencing those whispers.

On one occasion, negotiations between the two families swiftly escalated into a fiery dispute over finances and traditions. His aunt, who bridged both families, stepped in to mediate. She phoned me, urging me to reconsider the wedding. She accused his family of greed and suggested I should break it off. But yet again, I chose to ignore her warning. Drowning into my own emotions, I could not see things. Memories of my failed engagement flooded back, stirring up all my insecurities. I couldn't bear the thought of another broken engagement. What if I never found another man? Perhaps it was just his family causing strife, not him.

So, I pleaded with him over the phone to act. He tried to call my family and offered an apology on his own. And just like that, we were back on track. His apology was all it took for me and my family to forgive and forget and to proceed with our wedding plans as if nothing had happened.

The warning signs glared, waving frantically like red flags in the wind. Others around me tried to caution me, but I was consumed by the dream of a fairy tale ending. I had a chance to step away, to heed the nagging feeling that something was amiss, but I chose to bury it beneath optimism.

WHAT I KNOW NOW

1.RELATIONSHIPS ARE A TWO-WAY STREET: A healthy relationship is built on mutual effort and shared investment. For a relationship to truly flourish, both partners must contribute—whether through love, time, or emotional energy. It's only natural that these contributions may ebb and flow as life's challenges come and go. However, there must always be an underlying balance—a sense that both people are equally committed to nurturing the bond.

In my case, my family and I were the ones who constantly gave. We gave our time, love, and resources, and often, we sacrificed our own needs to ensure everything went smoothly for them. We adjusted our expectations and priorities to accommodate their situations, hoping they would appreciate our efforts and reciprocate. Instead of receiving respect, understanding, and effort, we faced a steady increase in demands. Each time we gave, it seemed to spark more requests, yet there was little to no return on that emotional investment.

This one-sided dynamic slowly started chipping away at the foundation of trust and respect that a healthy relationship is supposed to rest upon. It was like watching a beautiful structure slowly crumble—piece by piece, with no way to stop it. Slowly, I began to feel neglected and unappreciated. And as that neglect deepened, so did the emotional distance.

The relationship can't stay balanced long when one side isn't invested. It becomes fragile, built on the illusion of love and connection, while, in reality, it teeters on the edge of collapse. The bond weakens without an equal commitment from both sides, and what was once strong eventually crumbles. Loyalty, respect, and trust cannot survive when partners aren't equally invested. These values need nurturing from both, or they will wither away, leaving behind a hollow shell of what the relationship was meant to be.

2. WHAT YOU SEE NOW IS WHAT YOU GET LATER: Ignoring too many red flags in a relationship is never a good idea, no matter how strong the connection may seem. The signs are often there from the beginning, but we usually ignore them, hoping that, with time, things will get better or the issues magically disappear. In reality, the early stages of a relationship—when both people are still presenting their best selves—often reveal more about a person's true character than we realise. We're so caught up in the excitement of new love that we overlook the little things that cause discomfort or unease. But those small, subtle behaviours can grow into much more significant issues as time goes on, and that's when the cracks in the relationship start to show.

I remember vividly making excuses for my ex-husband. I saw the signs; my well-wishers kept pointing them out, but I kept convincing myself that things would improve. I told myself that, with time, he would change and become the partner I hoped for. But his actions never aligned with my long-term vision for us. I kept clinging to the belief that love could fix everything and that things would eventually get better with enough patience. However, I knew the truth: you can't change someone's fundamental nature. People are who they are, and no amount of hoping or wishing will alter their core values or behaviours.

In my case, I kept waiting for the man I dreamed of, but I was settling for someone who didn't align with my needs or aspirations. I made excuses for him, ignored the warning signs, and kept thinking that love would be enough to make everything right. But the reality is when someone's actions don't match their words, it's a sign that something isn't right. You can either accept them as they are or move on to find a partner whose values and actions align with yours from the start. You deserve someone whose behaviour matches their promises and whose commitment to you is unwavering, not someone who keeps falling short of the person they should be. No matter what you think, you deserve to be with someone who makes you feel loved, respected, and truly valued—right from the beginning.

5

LOSING MYSELF IN MARRIAGE

"Not until we are lost do we begin to find ourselves."
– Henry David Thoreau.

A. MY QUEST TO BE THE IDEAL WIFE

When our wedding day finally arrived, it felt like the end of one struggle and the beginning of a new chapter. Against all odds, we exchanged vows, and the months of anticipation and turmoil seemed to culminate in this one moment of relief. Shortly after the celebrations, we moved to the UK—a much-needed escape from the drama that had consumed me in the lead-up to the wedding.

But I didn't realise then that while I had left the chaos behind, I was walking into a new set of challenges—ones that would stretch my resilience and, more importantly, make me question who I was. The first few months in the UK were blissful. We were in the honeymoon phase, where everything felt easy as if I had found my soulmate. We spent so much time together, often just enjoying each other's company, and I felt a peace I hadn't felt in years. I kept thanking God for blessing me with such a wonderful husband. I truly believed our happiness would last forever.

We spent weeks together, exploring the country, learning about the UK lifestyle, and soaking in the beauty of this new chapter. Life felt promising, and I thought I had finally found the life I'd always wanted. But soon enough, the honeymoon phase began to fade, and reality crept in. I had left behind everything I knew—my family, my friends, the comfort of familiarity—and I was now trying to carve a new life in a foreign country. While his life stayed essentially the same, mine was completely uprooted. I had to learn to drive, take on new responsibilities, and start searching for a job. It felt like I was beginning from scratch in every aspect of my life.

Despite all the challenges, I dedicated myself entirely to my new role as a wife. I would dress up for him when he came home, cook his favourite meals, and create romantic settings to make him feel special. I believed that if I gave my all to our marriage, he would see my efforts and appreciate them.

But slowly, I began to realise that my efforts were going unnoticed. He would often work late, spend evenings out drinking with his colleagues, and call me at midnight, asking me to pick him up so he wouldn't have to pay for a taxi. My gestures were not being acknowledged, no matter how big or small. I was giving everything to the relationship, but I wasn't getting anything in return. Once again, I was investing more than he was, and it began to take its toll.

Over time, my initial enthusiasm started to fade. I could no longer maintain the image of the "perfect wife" I had created in my mind. I stopped dressing up, stopped cooking elaborate meals, and slowly withdrew from trying to make the home as perfect as I had once imagined. I wanted to earn his love by prioritising his needs over my own. But instead of feeling loved, I started feeling invisible.

All I wanted were small gestures showing me I was appreciated—a simple "thank you" or maybe a bouquet of flowers just because. I wanted to feel like my efforts were seen as I mattered. But those gestures were few and far between, and when they did come, they lacked consistency. I began to settle for the scraps of affection he offered, desperately trying to hold onto the hope that things would get better.

Months passed, and I still hadn't found a job. I had no life outside of the marriage. The loneliness and confusion began to suffocate me. I wasn't close to his family, and I didn't want to burden mine with my struggles, so I found myself once again isolated and alone.

I began to question everything. Was this just how things were in the UK—was going out drinking and expecting midnight rides home a cultural norm? Or was this just his behaviour, his personality? I couldn't figure out where the line between cultural differences and personal flaws began.

In my quest to be the "perfect wife," I had repeatedly lowered my expectations. I had convinced myself that if I sacrificed enough, I could create my dream marriage. But the truth is, I was losing myself. I was constantly putting his needs ahead of mine, and in doing so, I was abandoning my dreams, desires, and identity. My hopes for the life I wanted—the vacations, the career, the home I envisioned—were all cast aside in favour of his priorities. His career flourished while mine remained stagnant, and I began to lose sight of who I was.

I had become a shadow, unnoticed by him and, most tragically, by myself. Nobody, not even me, considered my needs, my dreams, or my identity. In trying so hard to fit into the mould of the "perfect wife," I had lost the person I once was.

B. A WAKE-UP CALL

By the second year of our marriage, we had already moved to a new town. The location was much better—there was more to do, and I felt more settled, though I was still struggling to find a proper job. Life seemed to be improving on the surface, but there was an underlying tension I couldn't quite place.

One evening, his hotel hosted a staff party, and partners were invited too. He had warned me that he'd be busy and unable to spend much time with me at the party. I didn't mind; I joined nevertheless and found myself seated with his general manager and wife at a table. He kept disappearing from the table, attending to various work-related things, and I found it hard to warm up to the people I was sitting with. The conversation was painfully formal and felt more like an obligation than a pleasant evening out.

I decided I wouldn't stay too long. Perhaps we could share a dance before I left, just to have a small moment together. So, I asked him to dance. He politely refused, telling me he had too much work and suggesting I head home without him. I understood and said my goodbyes to the few people I knew, making my way toward the car.

But as I walked to the car, I realised I'd left my purse in his office, which had the house keys inside. Frustrated, I turned back and headed toward the hotel.

As I walked into the party hall again, my eyes caught something that made my heart drop. He was on the dance floor, surrounded by his female staff, laughing and dancing like he didn't have a care in the world.

Minutes before, he had told me he was too busy to dance with me. Yet he was fully engaged with others while I was dismissed. My chest tightened with anger and hurt. I walked straight up to him, barely able to contain my rage, and asked him to unlock his office so I could retrieve my purse. I didn't hide my anger; my face must have been flushed red as I stood there.

He seemed taken aback but obliged, leading me back to his office while trying to explain himself. He said his staff had insisted he join them, that he didn't want to seem rude, and that's why he danced. But I didn't care. All I could think was that his staff mattered more to him than I did. His work life took precedence over our personal life—over me. I grabbed my purse and stormed out of the hotel, tears burning as I walked home.

When I got back, something inside me snapped. I realised that whilst I was married to him, he was still a bachelor at heart. I packed a bag, stuffed my belongings inside, and grabbed my passport. I was done. I was going to catch the next flight back to India. This wasn't the life I had signed up for. I sat down at the table and wrote a long letter explaining everything—how he had no sense of responsibility toward me, how he was still living like a bachelor, and how I could no longer tolerate it—two years of frustration poured out in a rush of anger, disappointment, and heartbreak.

With my bag in one hand and my passport in the other, I walked toward the door, fully prepared to leave. Just as I reached for the handle, the door flung open. There he was, standing in the doorway, his face pale and his eyes wide with panic. He must have sensed the seriousness of the situation.

I handed him the letter and told him I was leaving. He looked at it for a moment, then back at me, before pleading with me not to go. He promised he would change things, that he would do better. I don't remember exactly what part of his apology or his pleas made me reconsider, but it made me pause. Maybe it was hope, or it was the belief that things really could get better. Whatever it was, I chose to give him another chance. I decided to stay.

That night, I thought I had given him a wake-up call—that my actions would finally make him see how serious I was about the state of our marriage. But in hindsight, it wasn't him who needed to wake up. It was me. The universe offered me a way out, a chance to leave behind a situation that wasn't serving me, but I couldn't see it. I stayed, convincing myself that things would change.

I stayed too long. Far too long.

C. RESENTMENT REPLACED ROMANCE

After what I thought was a wake-up call, things changed, at least for a while. He started paying more attention to me, communicating better, and making more effort to help around the house. He cut back on his outings with friends and spent more time at home. I finally found a permanent job—one I was proud of—and life began to feel like it was back on track. With two incomes, money wasn't as tight, and we even bought our first home together.

But as time passed, resentment began to creep into our relationship, slowly but surely replacing the love and romance that once connected us. I felt like I was no longer a partner but a mere bystander in our marriage—insignificant, invisible. My unhappiness started to show through constant arguments, biting comments, and an increasing emotional distance between us. He even called me "Complain Register," as if my frustration was nothing more than a running joke, a reminder that I spoke up too often about my unhappiness.

Each fight felt like an internal war. My heart screamed that I was justified in my anger and had every right to feel the way I did. But my mind kept pushing me to fulfil the role I had created for myself—the understanding wife, the one who quietly endured, smoothed over the rough patches and kept the peace. I struggled to reconcile the two. The more I tried to live up to that ideal, the more I failed. My emotions felt like a constant tug-of-war with my logical mind.

Celebrations? They became meaningless. Diwali, New Year's, Valentine's Day—all these special days blurred into one long stretch of loneliness. His work always came first, even on Christmas. I would sit alone, telling myself that these moments didn't matter and that I needed to be more understanding of his busy schedule. But deep down, it broke me. Every missed celebration, every unacknowledged special occasion, chipped away at my sense of self-worth. It felt like I watched the world move forward while I remained stuck in place, convinced that this was simply what it meant to be a "good wife."

In a desperate attempt to maintain some semblance of peace, I became the one to apologise after every argument, even when I knew I wasn't at fault. But the more I apologised, the heavier my heart grew. I would come home from work to an empty house, only to face chores and the deafening silence that felt like a weight on my chest. Attending pregnancy classes alone was particularly low. His absence reminded me how little I seemed to matter in his world.

With every unspoken word, every lonely night, resentment continued to build until the love and empathy I once had for him began to fade. I was trapped in a constant disappointment cycle, unable to escape. On the rare occasions when he did something thoughtful—like buying a gift or taking me out for dinner—I would cling to those moments as if they were lifelines, desperate to feel valued. But those gestures were fleeting, like scraps of affection that never lasted. I often heard the same painful words: "You don't understand me" or "You never support me." Those words became a constant hum in the background of our life, ringing in my ears long after they were spoken.

In the quiet corners of my mind, I began keeping score. Every argument, every time I gave more than I received, every special occasion spent alone added to the growing list of grievances I carried with me. I grew bitter, angry, and resentful. The smile that had once come so naturally disappeared. I no longer cared to put in the effort. I went through the motions, doing what was expected of me—cooking, cleaning, playing the role of the "good wife"—while feeling like a ghost in my home.

I felt trapped and helpless. I would often threaten to leave, but deep down, I knew I had already accepted this as my reality. This was what marriage had become—a shadow of my envisioned life. The idea of happiness felt distant, like a memory from a life I had once known but could never return to.

D. HIS DREAM BECAME MY DREAM

While my career had become solid, it always played second fiddle to his. Every time he needed to move for work, I adjusted, changing jobs to support his career trajectory. My life began to feel like a series of sacrifices for his success.

He often complained about how much he hated his long hours at work and dreamed of starting his own business. He yearned for more freedom, to create something of his own. So, when I inherited some money a few years later, I decided to invest in his dream.

We excitedly began to explore opportunities in the hospitality industry and eventually decided to open a café. Together, we built its identity, leased space, and poured our hearts into making it work. The first few months were tough, as most businesses struggled initially, but eventually, the café started to break even. This was a small victory because we didn't have to pump any more of our finances into it. I was just as involved as he was, working hard alongside my full-time job, dedicating my evenings and weekends to support his dream.

But running a business is far from easy—it requires resilience, grit, and mental strength. As the stress of long hours, tough competition, and the weight of a fixed-term lease mounted, I could see it taking a toll on him. He began to struggle, mentally and emotionally. He missed his old life—the polished image of wearing "Armani suits" and managing teams in 5-star hotels. The café, with its constant demands and modest returns, felt like a burden.

While he wrestled with the challenges of the café, I was battling my difficulties at work. My relationship with my manager had soured, so my job became unbearable. I'd come home in tears, completely drained, desperately wanting to quit. But he insisted I keep working. "We need the security of a steady income," he would say, urging me to "suck it up." After months of enduring a toxic work environment, I reached my breaking point. I couldn't take it anymore. I started voicing my frustration, accusing him of caring only about the money and not about me or my well-being.

In response, almost as if to prove he did care, he finally said, "Fine, if you're that unhappy, then quit." So, I did. I resigned, thinking that at least this would bring me some peace.

Yet, his longing to return to his old life intensified. He felt trapped in the café, disillusioned with the entrepreneurial dream he once chased. He decided to sell the business. I suggested ways to save the company and pleaded not to sell, offering to run the cafe myself. But he lashed out, saying, "You don't support me."

He soon found a buyer and sold the business at a loss, causing me to lose my entire investment. But what hurt far more than the money was the blame that followed. Instead of acknowledging the sacrifices I had made—financially, emotionally, and physically—he accused me of pushing him into the venture he did not want.

That was when the painful truth began to dawn on me. I sacrificed my career, health, happiness, and identity to realise my husband's dream. I had bent over backwards, putting his needs and desires before my own, time and time again. And yet, it was never enough. Instead of gratitude, he blamed me. Instead of love, he accused me.

The realisation crushed me. I had poured everything into a relationship that only took from me. His dream had consumed my life, and in the end, I was left feeling exhausted, frustrated, and utterly broken.

WHAT I KNOW NOW

1. YOU ARE RESPONSIBLE FOR YOUR HAPPINESS: In my effort to be the perfect wife, I gave until I had nothing left. I kept pouring from an empty cup, thinking I could continue without refilling it. I focused so much on fulfilling his needs, thinking he would do the same for me, that I neglected my own. I could create harmony in our relationship by sacrificing my desires, opinions, and happiness. But the truth is, you cannot give from an empty cup.

Eventually, I reached the point of burnout. The resentment that had quietly built up over time started to take its toll on both of us. I didn't realise how crucial it was to nurture myself and prioritise my needs. It took far too long to realise that I needed to fill my cup first to continue giving to others.

Emotionally, I relied on him for everything. I expected him to be my family, friend, and lover—essentially, my everything. I was waiting for him to meet the emotional needs I should have been able to meet for myself. This created an unhealthy dynamic in our relationship. I placed immense pressure on him, expecting him to fulfil all my needs while failing to recognise the importance of nurturing my own sense of self.

What I learned the hard way is that a healthy relationship is built on two whole individuals, not one person trying to meet every need of the other. Having your own life—friends, hobbies, passions, and independence—allows you to maintain a sense of self and balance in the relationship. It's important not to lose yourself in your partner. Instead, you should grow together while still keeping your identities intact. Only then can you indeed show up for each other in meaningful ways.

2. I TAUGHT HIM HOW TO TREAT ME: The way we allow others to treat us is often a direct reflection of what we accept from them. The more we give without boundaries, the more others take. In hindsight, I failed to set boundaries early on. I constantly said yes, even when I didn't want to. Whether waiting for him to come home late, picking him up in the middle of the night, or going along with whatever he needed, I always complied without hesitation.

By doing this, I unintentionally taught him that his behaviour was acceptable. I didn't set clear expectations for how I wanted to be treated, so he kept pushing those boundaries. But it wasn't just him; I also failed to communicate my needs and limitations. I thought that if I just endured, things would improve. I expected him to automatically understand what upset me or how I wanted to be treated. Instead, I ended up enabling the very behaviours that hurt me.

A healthy relationship thrives on mutual respect; boundaries are essential to maintaining that respect. Without them, the foundation of the relationship weakens. I now understand the importance of clearly communicating what is acceptable and what isn't. Expressing your needs openly is crucial because, if you don't, how can you expect them to be met?

3. HE WAS EMOTIONALLY ABSENT: If your partner can watch you cry and ignore you if you are constantly begging for communication. However, he avoids it because he doesn't want to argue if he can fall asleep soundly while you're still upset—then, sadly, he doesn't love you anymore. Worse, he may never have loved you the way you needed. Love isn't just about the happy moments or the occasional romantic gesture—it's about being there for each other, especially during tough times.

I often cried when I was upset, and more often than not, my tears went unnoticed. If I didn't cry, I'd get angry and demand a conversation, but instead of the comfort and support I needed, he would dismiss it with, "Not now; I don't want to get into an argument." I was left feeling invisible and unheard. He was emotionally absent, utterly detached from my pain, while I was left to carry it on my own.

Love requires emotional engagement, understanding, and empathy. When your partner is emotionally absent during vulnerable moments, that's a huge red flag. In a healthy, loving relationship, your partner should listen, comfort, and try to resolve issues. But when the emotional bond fades, and you're left begging for communication, it's clear that something is broken.

The final blow is when, even after a difficult conversation, he falls asleep soundly, unaffected by the weight of the emotional turmoil. That's not love—it's indifference. It's as if your feelings no longer matter. If your partner can let you go to bed in tears, not because he's unaware, but because he doesn't care, then love is no longer present in the relationship.

At that point, you're not in a partnership. You're just two people coexisting in the same space but emotionally distant. Love is supposed to be a shared journey, but the bond dissolves when one partner stops showing up emotionally. That's when you realise that the love you thought you had may have never indeed been there in the first place.

6

SEXUAL STIGMA AND INTIMACY

"It's not about being sexy, it's about being confident and me being confident in my sexuality."

A. SEX STIGMATISED

In India, sex is often surrounded by stigma despite the country's historical and cultural connection to the Kama Sutra. This ancient text celebrates the art of love and sexual pleasure. There was a time in Indian history when sex was viewed openly and positively as a natural and beautiful part of human life. Temples across the country are adorned with intricate sculptures depicting erotic imagery, symbolising the celebration of human sexuality. Yet, today, the narrative around sex has dramatically shifted.

In modern India, sex is often treated as a taboo subject. Various factors, including religion, colonial history, societal norms, gender dynamics, and political views, influence this. The result is a widespread sense of shame and discomfort surrounding sexual expression. I felt this stigma acutely as I grew up. Sex education in schools was either non-existent or very limited, and even at home, there was little to no open conversation about sex or sexual health. Sexual desires and behaviours were often associated with shame, making it difficult to feel comfortable with the subject or to express any curiosity or need related to it.

In my own family, public displays of affection were strongly discouraged. Affection was something that seemed hidden away, never openly expressed. I don't recall my parents or extended family ever holding hands or showing love openly in front of others. Physical contact beyond a specific limit is seen as inappropriate, and any form of affection, like a simple hug or holding hands, will often draw judgment or disapproval. I was raised in an environment where no one, including my parents, ever said "I love you." While not every Indian household shares this experience, it significantly shaped my views on affection and intimacy.

This toxic mix of feeling unattractive and growing up with rigid, conservative beliefs about what was acceptable regarding sex turned me into a closed-off person. Even with friends, something as simple as hugging made me uncomfortable. I rarely initiated physical contact and felt overwhelming discomfort when someone hugged me. I had built emotional walls so high that I often felt isolated and disconnected from others, even when surrounded by people who cared for me.

I often wondered what it would be like to be in a relationship, to feel physically comfortable being close to a man finally. I imagined what it would be like to experience intimacy without the weight of shame and confusion that I carried. But the reality was far from what I had hoped. My silence about my sexuality and the overwhelming difficulty I had discussing or engaging in sexual matters haunted me for years. I struggled to understand my sexual needs and desires, let alone express them to anyone. This lack of understanding made me feel disconnected from my body and emotions.

The first time I brought up the topic of sex with my mother was when I was 24 and already engaged to be married. Looking back, it felt tragically late. By this time, I had learned everything I knew about sex from friends, magazines, and the occasional glimpse into a TV show or movie. When I walked down the aisle at 25, I was still a virgin, holding onto a sense of pride in that status. But beneath that pride was a storm of confusion, fear, and anxiety. I didn't know what to expect in my married life nor how to navigate the intimacy I was about to face. The emotional baggage I carried left me unprepared for the realities of intimacy, and I quickly realised that sex was more complicated than I had imagined.

This experience has shaped my understanding of sex and intimacy as a deeply personal and complex journey. For so many people, especially women, societal pressures and cultural stigmas make it incredibly difficult to explore and express their sexuality. The shame surrounding sex, particularly in a culture like mine, can lead to years of confusion, self-doubt, and isolation. It took me years to unlearn many of these ingrained beliefs and start understanding what a healthy sexual life looks like.

B. LOVE LANGUAGES LOST IN TRANSLATION

My stigma around sex kept me from confidently taking the lead in our relationship. The deep-seated shame and discomfort I carried about sex made it difficult for me to step into a more active and engaged role in our intimate life, despite my efforts to learn and understand the subject through countless books and articles. I was constantly preoccupied with worries about how I looked, whether I was desirable, and if I was doing things "right." These concerns became an invisible wall between me and my husband, preventing me from fully embracing and enjoying our connection.

Whenever I mustered the courage to take the initiative physically, the moments were often met with rejection, and each rejection felt like a painful reinforcement of my insecurities. Instead of trying again, I withdrew further into my shell, believing that I wasn't enough and that my desires weren't valid. This silence around my feelings only added to the growing distance between us. The emotional disconnect, paired with my constant doubts about myself, made it nearly impossible to navigate the complexities of intimacy in our relationship.

Our differences in love languages only complicated the situation. I expressed love through acts of service, caring for the home, helping with tasks, and showing my affection by taking care of his needs. On the other hand, my husband's love language was physical touch. He sought connection through physical closeness—holding hands, cuddling, or being near each other. He would reach for my hand when we went out, but I rarely reciprocated with the same enthusiasm. My hand would often lie limp in his, which would frustrate him. He would complain about it, but I never knew how to express that it wasn't that I didn't love him; it was that I wasn't comfortable with physical affection. In the early days, no matter where, he would find ways to have physical touch, even if his arms touched mine.

Unknowingly, his need for physical closeness was lost on me, while every effort I made to show love through caring actions seemed to go unnoticed. It felt like the love I was offering was invisible to him. My heart grew heavy with the feeling that I was failing him while his silent frustrations about the lack of intimacy quietly built up. These unspoken frustrations created an emotional storm, and neither knew how to navigate it. I craved emotional connection before physical intimacy, while he longed for physical closeness.

As life became busier and the demands of everyday living increased, our relationship began to shift. Intimacy faded into the background, pushed aside by responsibilities and obligations. When I became pregnant, the physical distance between us grew even more. We had no physical closeness for nearly a year, and what had once been a warm, affectionate bond started to feel cold and distant. I didn't realise it then, but I was pushing him away. My insecurity and doubts built invisible walls that became harder to break down as time passed.

We weren't speaking each other's love languages, and my growing self-doubt slowly seeped into every corner of our marriage like poison. The more disconnected we became, the more resentment began to build, and it hung over us like an ever-present dark cloud. We stopped trying to understand each other's needs, and the emotional and physical intimacy that had once connected us seemed out of reach.

I often wonder whether our love faded because our intimacy disappeared or if the lack of intimacy was a result of a lack of love. There's still a nagging feeling I can't shake—about the pride I felt in being a virgin when we got married, thinking it was a virtue. But perhaps that pride led him to see me differently, maybe even with less respect. I can't help but wonder if my lack of sexual confidence and my inability to embrace my sexuality entirely played a key role in the unravelling of our relationship.

Looking back, I question if things could have been different if I had been more self-assured and if I had embraced my desires and fears.

Could I have changed the course of our relationship by letting go of the insecurities that held me back? Would things have been different if I had learned to communicate better about my needs and accepted my sexuality without shame? These questions linger, and they still shape how I view my role in the downfall of what we once had.

WHAT I KNOW NOW

1. SELF-PERCEPTION SHAPES INTIMACY: How you see yourself profoundly influences how you show up in intimate moments with your partner. If you're constantly battling insecurities or lack confidence in your body, it can create emotional barriers that make it challenging to engage in intimate experiences fully. Intimacy is about more than physical closeness—it's about allowing yourself to be seen and accepted by your partner.

When you struggle with negative self-perception, it becomes hard to be emotionally available, to express your desires, or even to enjoy the connection. You're more focused on your perceived flaws than being present with the person you love. The anxiety about being judged or not be

But it changes everything when you start to embrace your body, accept yourself for who you are, and develop a positive relationship with yourself. You can confidently step into intimate moments, ready to engage openly and authentically. It allows you to connect on a much deeper level—emotionally, physically, and spiritually. Feeling good in your skin makes you more likely to express your needs and desires without hesitation, fostering trust and emotional safety. Intimacy becomes more than just an exchange; it becomes a mutual journey of connection, vulnerability, and love.

Your self-perception directly shapes the quality of your relationships and intimacy. If you can love and accept yourself, you'll be able to offer and receive love in a more fulfilling, open, and authentic way.

2. MEN AND WOMEN EXPRESS LOVE DIFFERENTLY: Men and women often express love in ways that can be confusing if we don't understand each other's needs. While women may express love emotionally through nurturing gestures, deep conversations, and acts of service, men often express love through physical intimacy. This difference can sometimes create tension in a relationship if both partners don't recognise and honour these varying expressions of affection.

Women, especially in committed relationships, seek emotional closeness and connection first. We crave open communication, understanding, and the emotional security of sharing our thoughts, feelings, and vulnerabilities. This emotional bond provides a sense of safety and intimacy, which makes us feel loved and valued. For women, love is often expressed through actions that demonstrate care, attention, and emotional support.

On the other hand, men tend to connect through physical intimacy— holding hands, hugging, kissing, and, of course, sexual connection. These physical expressions of affection are their way of showing love, creating a sense of closeness and bonding. For many men, physical touch is a direct line to emotional connection. When they reach for you, hold you, or make physical advances, it's their way of saying, "I care about you," "I want to be close to you," or "You matter to me."

This difference can create frustration if it's not understood. Women may feel neglected if their partner isn't offering the emotional intimacy they desire, while men may feel rejected if their physical gestures aren't reciprocated or appreciated. Both forms of intimacy are necessary, and finding a balance that works for both partners is essential.

When we understand that our partner's way of expressing love might differ, we can approach each other with greater empathy and patience. Instead of assuming a lack of love, we can recognise these differences as part of our relationship's unique dynamic, making space for emotional and physical intimacy to thrive. We can deepen our bond and strengthen our connection by learning to meet each other's needs in ways that resonate with both partners.

3. INTIMACY IS A JOURNEY; GROWING TOGETHER MATTERS:
Intimacy does not happen overnight; it requires both partners to grow together. If two people are genuinely committed to each other, they will find a way to make their relationship work, even through chal-

lenges. However, being on the same page and sharing the same values is essential.

In my relationship, I often wondered whether the lack of intimacy led to the loss of love or if there was never any love, to begin with to sustain the intimacy.

What I know for sure is that things were not meant to happen the way they did. I was inexperienced when it came to intimacy, while he was more knowledgeable. I did not know what I did not know. If he truly cared, he could have taken me on that journey with him, held my hand, and shown me the way. Instead, he chose to leave me behind, making no effort to nurture our emotional bond. We weren't growing together, and it became clear that our relationship was not built on mutual understanding or shared growth.

My pride in being a virgin when we married may have led him to view me as inexperienced or even undesirable, creating a divide between us. Our differing experiences and values prevented us from connecting in a meaningful way. Intimacy requires patience, communication, and a willingness to grow together as a couple. Without these, it becomes difficult to build a strong, lasting connection.

7

MOTHERHOOD

"Motherhood is the greatest thing and the hardest thing"
- Ricki Lake

A. PREGNANCY IN SILENCE

Four years into our marriage, life settled into a predictable routine. His odd working hours remained constant, but we had fallen into an unspoken pattern. Weekends were divided between me cooking elaborate meals on one day and dining out on the other; he cooked on rare occasions. Vacations were infrequent, with a modest holiday every couple of years. On the surface, we appeared to have a stable life, both holding decent jobs. Yet beneath it all, I felt a growing ache—a profound yearning to become a mother. My husband, however, didn't share this desire. While he wasn't opposed to the idea, he lacked the passion I felt so profoundly. Ultimately, he gave in—not from a place of shared longing but under the weight of familial expectations.

I immersed myself in the process, buying countless tests to track ovulation and diligently monitoring my body. As each month came to an end, I would anxiously take pregnancy tests, waiting for that life-changing moment. Finally, one test came back positive. My heart raced joyfully as I rushed to tell my husband the news. "I'm pregnant!" I announced, expecting shared elation. His response was a simple, "Oh, okay."

I couldn't understand his lack of enthusiasm. Perhaps he wasn't surprised, given all our efforts, or maybe he needed time to process it. Whatever the reason, I refused to let it dampen my excitement. The joy of bringing new life inside me made me feel invincible as if nothing else mattered.

But that happiness was fleeting. Just weeks into the pregnancy, one evening at the movies, I began to bleed. I tried to convince myself that it was nothing serious, but deep down, I felt the dread creeping in. The next day, my worst fears were confirmed—I had lost the baby. My world crumbled as I spent the day in tears, feeling hollow and defeated. Yet, this tragedy only fuelled my desire for a child even more.

After allowing my body time to recover, we tried again. Just a few months later, I took another test—and it was positive. Ecstatic doesn't even begin to describe how I felt. The shadow of sadness over me seemed to dissolve, replaced by an overwhelming surge of hope. I was ready to embrace this pregnancy wholeheartedly. At the same time, my job had become increasingly stressful, and maintaining a good relationship with my manager felt like an uphill battle. Recognising the toll it was taking, I decided to quit. I wanted to dedicate myself fully to this child and this journey, giving it my undivided attention.

With our families living in India and few friends nearby, a baby shower or celebration seemed out of reach. I was isolated, with no job and few people around to share this precious journey. My mum visited us often but couldn't live with us for long. I relied on my husband for company and support, but his work often consumed him. On his days off, he tried—he cooked my favourite meals, cleaned the house, and sat with me when he could. His efforts were genuine, but they were brief respites in my days' long stretches of loneliness.

I sought community by joining clubs and classes for expectant mothers, attending everything from parental guidance sessions to workshops designed for expecting couples. Yet, my husband never joined me; he was always too busy, and I rarely asked him to come, still trapped by the need to be the "perfect wife." I didn't want to burden him, even though I carried the emotional weight of doing it alone.

During one of these classes, I looked around at the other couples, watching them share intimate smiles, laughter, and tender support.

That's when the full weight of my isolation hit me. While they were navigating this journey together, I was doing it alone. I left the class feeling emptier than ever, realising how distant I felt from my husband in this most vulnerable time of our lives.

I started asking for more of his presence, but I don't think I ever truly expressed the depth of my need. I was careful not to make demands or disrupt his busy schedule. Even when my pregnancy became more challenging, I couldn't shake the feeling that his job—and everything else—was more important than me and our unborn child. I buried my hurt, letting the "perfect wife" syndrome take over once again. And as I silently carried the weight of my emotions, the distance between us grew wider.

B. NEW BEGINNINGS, NEW CHALLENGES

Though fraught with complications, the nine months of pregnancy passed in a whirlwind of preparation and excitement. We poured our energy into decorating the nursery, carefully choosing every baby essential, and spending countless hours debating names we both adored. Despite the emotional distance that had grown between my husband and me, these small moments of planning felt like fleeting sparks of connection in an otherwise strained relationship.

The journey, however, was anything but smooth. I battled constant sickness for the first six months, with frequent hospital visits becoming a part of my routine. Yet, as soon as I felt my daughter's tiny movements, everything shifted. Those gentle flutters filled me with an indescribable sense of joy and anticipation. She seemed to come alive whenever I watched cricket, her kicks as though cheering along with me, and I lovingly joked about her "kisses from the inside." My favourite movie at the time was *Independence Day*, and it felt serendipitous when complications led to her early arrival—on the 4th of July, no less.

Her arrival via emergency C-section was both nerve-wracking and miraculous. Holding my baby for the first time felt like the world stopped, and in that moment, all the pain and struggles of the past months dissolved. Yet, the joy was short-lived. She was rushed to the ICU due to unstable blood sugar levels, and instead of bringing her home to the nursery we had lovingly prepared, I spent the next week by her side in the hospital. Sleepless nights blurred into one another as I watched her tiny body in the incubator, praying for her recovery and dreading the moments I had to leave her.

Finally, after a week, we were allowed to bring her home. My mother and brother prepared a warm welcome, decorated the house, and filled it with love and laughter. Yet, the challenges of motherhood soon set in. After a month, my mum returned to India, leaving me to navigate the uncharted waters of early motherhood alone. My hormones were a mess, and with my husband consumed by his demanding job, I had no one to lean on. Though he tried to help in his way, his long hours kept him primarily absent, and even when he was there, his comfort felt distant. We both carried the weight of this life-altering experience, but it often felt like we were doing so separately.

In those early months, my daughter became the centre of my world. I bathed, played with her, and immersed myself in the rollercoaster of sleepless nights and hormonal chaos. Yet, none of it mattered compared to the sheer joy of having her. Her laughter filled my heart, and her cries tugged at my soul. For the first time, I felt a profound connection with another human being—a bond that was both a blessing and a revelation. I watched in awe as she grew from a tiny, fragile baby to a curious, vibrant little girl. Her first words, wobbly steps, and blossoming personality were moments that were etched into my heart.

But even as I poured myself into motherhood, the cracks in my relationship with my husband grew wider. When she was seven months old, I returned to work, hoping to regain balance. My days became a relentless routine of dropping her at daycare, working long hours, and returning home to cook, clean, and prepare her for bed. My husband insisted I needed to work for the financial stability it provided, but society's whispers—that she was too young to be apart from me—only deepened my guilt.

I tried to do everything: maintaining a spotless home, cooking healthy meals, and ensuring my daughter thrived in every way possible. But the weight of these expectations became overwhelming. The exhaustion seeped into my temperament, and even minor mishaps—like my daughter spilling water—would ignite waves of frustration. To cope, I began avoiding activities that might create more mess or chaos, unknowingly stifling her natural curiosity and creativity.

Weeks turned into months; before I knew it, my tiny baby had grown into a vibrant five-year-old. She was maturing faster than I imagined—a bright, curious, and independent little girl. Yet, in my relentless quest to maintain control amidst the chaos of life, I had unknowingly become an overbearing mother. My need for order and perfection had taken precedence, leaving little room for spontaneity or exploration. Looking back, I realised that while I had given her all of me, I had also unknowingly held her back in ways I never intended.

C. THE MIRROR EFFECT

Motherhood had turned into a journey of revelations, each more profound than the last. As I immersed myself in raising my daughter, I noticed something unsettling yet familiar—I was seeing reflections of my mother in myself. Without even realising it, I had adopted her parenting style, echoing her habits, reactions, and even her quirks. The things that once frustrated me about my mother were now reappearing in my actions, almost as if I had unknowingly been programmed to repeat them.

It wasn't intentional. It felt as though I was running on autopilot, my parenting choices driven by the deeply ingrained patterns I had grown up with. Despite my best efforts to carve out my own identity as a mother, I had unknowingly inherited her worldview—her way of navigating challenges, her manner of expressing love, and, most uncomfortably, her fears.

The most startling realisation came when my daughter began to speak. Her first words were endearing, but as her vocabulary grew, I started to hear echoes of myself. Phrases I used daily slipped effortlessly from her lips, often accompanied by the same tone and expressions I unknowingly employed. She wasn't just mimicking my words—she was embodying my mannerisms and mirroring my behaviours.

This went beyond language. My fears, anxieties, and insecurities were subtly but surely becoming hers. I had always harboured an intense fear of insects, and without ever intending to, I had passed this on to her. Soon, I found her reacting to the sight of a harmless bug with the same apprehension I did. My hesitations around strangers, my cautiousness in unfamiliar settings—every unspoken cue I gave shaped her perception of the world.

It was both humbling and terrifying. I had always wanted to raise my daughter to be fearless and free-spirited, yet here she was, absorbing my strengths and the fears I had spent a lifetime trying to overcome. She was a mirror reflecting the parts of myself I had ignored, suppressed, or never thought were visible to others.

Every smile, frown, word, and sigh of frustration became a part of her growing consciousness. I realised that my role as a mother wasn't just about teaching or protecting her; it was also about unlearning my negative patterns so that I didn't unknowingly pass them on. She wasn't just watching me; she was becoming me in ways that felt both beautiful and daunting.

It became clear that I held immense power to nurture her with love and guidance and inadvertently pass on my unresolved fears and struggles. The responsibility weighed heavily on me. If I wanted her to grow into her unique person, unburdened by my past, I needed to confront the parts of myself I had long avoided.

The journey of motherhood, I realised, was as much about shaping her as it was about reshaping myself. I couldn't escape the generational echoes of my upbringing, but I could learn to recognise them and choose a different path. For her sake, I had to become the version of myself I wanted her to reflect—a mother who could acknowledge her flaws but still strive for growth, offering her daughter a legacy of strength, self-awareness, and love.

WHAT I KNOW NOW

1. A SPOTLESS HOME WON'T EARN ME AN AWARD: For years, I believed that a clean, organised house reflected my worth as a wife and mother. I would push myself to exhaustion, scrubbing floors, rearranging cupboards, and ensuring every room looked perfect. I thought maintaining this image of perfection meant I was doing things right. But I've learned that no one is handing out awards for spotless homes. My daughter won't remember how sparkling the floors were or how neatly the cushions were arranged. She will remember the times we played hide-and-seek in a messy living room, baked cookies together in a flour-dusted kitchen, or stayed up late watching movies with toys scattered around us.

I realised that in my quest for a perfect home, I was missing out on simple, meaningful moments with her. Now, I'm learning to let go of the need for everything to be perfect and to embrace the messiness of life. Because in the end, what truly matters isn't the spotless house—it's the laughter, connection, and memories we create together.

2. RAISING A HAPPY CHILD STARTS WITH A HAPPY PARENT:
For the longest time, I believed that being a "good mother" meant sacrificing my dreams, interests, and identity. I felt like I had to put everything I wanted on hold to focus solely on my child. Anytime I craved even a moment for myself—to read a book, pursue a hobby, or sit quietly—I felt an overwhelming sense of guilt. I thought that prioritising myself was selfish and somehow made me inadequate as a mother. But now I know the truth: sacrificing my happiness doesn't make me a better parent—it makes me exhausted and unhappy.
My child truly needs a happy, present, and authentic mom—not a perfect one.

My career was something I worked hard for, and as it grew, it brought opportunities to travel and experience new things. Many people dream of having a career like mine that allows me to learn, grow, and see the world. But every time I packed my bags for a trip, whether for a day or a week, guilt weighed heavily on my heart. The thought of leaving my daughter behind filled me with anxiety. I couldn't fully enjoy the opportunities or celebrate my achievements because of this nagging voice in my head that told me I was failing as a mother.

I now see things differently. My daughter doesn't need me to be with her every second, nor does she need me to sacrifice my happiness for hers. She truly needs to see me living my life fully and authentically. By embracing my career and following my passions, I am showing her that having your dreams is okay, even as a parent. When I honour my own needs and pursue the things that make me happy, I give her permission to do the same in her life.

I hope that as she grows, she understands that she doesn't have to fit into a mould or follow what others think is "right." She can forge her path, make choices, and embrace a life that fulfils her. By living authentically and unapologetically, I'm paving the way for her to feel free to do the same.

Being a mother isn't about abandoning yourself. It's about finding balance—being present for your child while also being present for yourself. When I show up for my life with joy and purpose and guilt-free, I give her the greatest gift: a role model who demonstrates that happiness and fulfilment are within reach for both of us

3. CHILDREN LEARN THROUGH WHAT THEY SEE, NOT JUST WHAT YOU SAY: One of the most eye-opening realisations I've had as a parent is that children absorb more from what they observe than their instructions. My daughter mirrors me in the words I speak and how I act, react, and even carry myself. I could tell her a hundred times not to fear bugs, but the moment she saw me jump at the sight of one, her fear was sealed. My actions spoke louder than my reassurances.

If I want my daughter to grow confident, kind, and resilient, I must embody those qualities. Words alone won't teach her; she's learning from my daily actions—big and small.

As a teenager, I prided myself on being independent and strong-willed. I had my thoughts and opinions about the world, and I couldn't care less about what my mother thought of me then. Yet, as I grew older and married, I subconsciously adopted her way of being a wife. She had become my silent role model for what a wife "should" be.

But in following her example, I unknowingly lost my sense of identity in my marriage. I didn't know how to be myself. When I became a mother, the same pattern repeated. Without explicit instructions, I adopted her parenting style almost on autopilot. Despite having strong opinions about how I thought she should have parented me, I found myself echoing her words, habits, and even frustrations in my motherhood journey.

This realisation was humbling. It showed me how deeply our children internalise what they see, even when they resist it. As I unknowingly modelled my mother's behaviour, my daughter is already watching and absorbing mine. Who I am now—how I respond to stress, treat others, and carry myself—will shape her view of the world and her role within it.

At some point in her life, she will look back and draw from my example, just as I did with my mother. It's a reminder that every action I take, every word I say, and even the energy I bring into a room leaves an imprint on her. She is not just learning from me but becoming a reflection of who I am.

8

SEPARATION

"There ain't no way you can hold onto something that wants to go."

A. WHEN THE UNIVERSE IS LISTENING TO YOU

Our differences became more apparent once he sold his business and took a job with a well-known budget hotel chain in the UK. The shift in his career marked a turning point, and the resentment quietly building over our nine years together reached its peak. I was emotionally exhausted—drained by the constant feeling of giving my all and receiving only blame in return. The weight of our dynamic was suffocating, and I yearned for change, for relief from the relentless burden of dissatisfaction.

I decided to stop sacrificing the small things I used to dismiss as inconsequential. Whether it was choosing the destination for our holidays or selecting the colour of the curtains in the living room, I started voicing my preferences. These seemingly trivial matters had once felt unimportant, but they represented more significant aspects of my sense of self.

As I began to assert myself, our disagreements intensified. We argued frequently, and in moments of frustration, I would threaten to leave, though I never followed through. Still, each argument exposed the stark contrast in our personalities, values, and aspirations.

I longed for adventure and new experiences, eagerly embracing the risks that came with them. On the other hand, my husband had a low tolerance for uncertainty, prioritising financial security above all else. I dreamed of expanding our family and having a second child, but he valued his freedom and resisted the idea, feeling that it would tie him down even further.

These differences weren't just surface-level disagreements but deep-rooted divides in our goals, values, and visions for the future. With each passing day, the gap between us widened, creating an unspoken tension that quietly infiltrated every aspect of our relationship.

I started to see how incompatible we had become.

One day, after he returned from a business trip, I was unpacking his suitcase and came across a toiletry kit with condoms inside. Confused and caught off guard, I asked him about it. His response was casual, almost dismissive: "Oh, it's just part of those hotel kits they leave as a standard in the room." His tone was so matter-of-fact that I chose to believe him, shrugging it off and filing it away as an odd but honest explanation.

Weeks later, we found ourselves in yet another argument. It was so petty that I can't even remember what started it. But what should have been a minor disagreement spiralled into a three-day standoff filled with tension and silence. He seemed indifferent, unwilling to engage or reconcile, leaving me angrier and more desperate with every attempt to mend the rift. It felt as if he was using the fight as an excuse to widen the growing chasm between us.

On the third day, I couldn't take it anymore. His cold resistance and lack of care were too much to bear. In pure frustration, I grabbed my coat and stormed out of the house, tears streaming down my face. My heart was pounding with the ache of rejection as I wandered into the woods, seeking solace in the silence of nature. I must have looked utterly unhinged as he followed me, clearly worried I might do something reckless or irrational.

I wandered deeper into the forest, the stillness amplifying the storm inside me. My tears mixed with sweat as I let out my anguish, yelling into the empty woods. "I can't do this anymore!" I cried, my voice breaking. "Please, change something! I can't live like this!" My words hung in the air, unanswered, as I collapsed onto the ground, exhausted and defeated.

I trudged through the trees for hours, my legs aching and my mind racing, until reality pulled me back. As much as I wanted to run away from my pain, I couldn't leave my daughter. She needed me, and that thought alone guided me back home.

As I walked through the door, he said bluntly, "I want a divorce," his words cutting deeper than any argument we'd ever had.

My chest tightened, my vision blurred. "Why?" I managed to whisper, my voice trembling with fear. Deep down, I had always feared this moment, but hearing it out loud made it all too real.

His answer was brutal, cutting me to the core. "I can't live with you anymore. It's too hard. You're always so angry and don't look good anymore. I just can't take it."

I stared at him, disbelief and devastation washing over me. I felt exposed like and stripped of every ounce of dignity. "Is there someone else?" I asked, my voice barely audible.

He met my gaze without flinching. "Of course not! You know me. If there were someone else, I'd tell you. It's just… we're not compatible anymore. I find it hard to be with you."

Despite the cruelty of his words, I believed him. I felt that this was my fault—that I had failed as a wife and partner. His accusations buried my heart, making me feel small, unworthy, and irreparably broken.

In that moment, the weight of our years together—the sacrifices, the arguments, the unspoken pain—came crashing down. The signs had been there all along, but I had ignored them, burying my fears beneath the hope that things would improve. Now, standing in the wreckage of our marriage, I couldn't deny the truth: everything was falling apart.

I crawled into bed that night, the tears coming in waves, soaking the pillow beneath me. I clung to the faint hope that this was just another fight, that by morning, he would change his mind, and things would return to the fragile normal we had grown used to. But deep down, I knew this wasn't just another fight. This was the end of the life I had known.

It felt that the universe had been listening to my cries in the woods. When I begged for change, it answered—just not in the way I had hoped. Sometimes, the change we desperately seek comes in forms that break us before they can heal us.

B. WHEN HOPE FIGHTS REALITY

The following day, I woke up with a tear-soaked pillow and swollen eyes, feeling utterly defeated. My reflection in the mirror looked as broken as I felt inside. A part of me clung desperately to the hope that this was just a bad dream or a passing phase and that things would somehow return to normal. I couldn't believe what was happening, and yet, I was drowning in the reality of it.

In my desperation, I begged him for answers, for something to hold on to. But his response was cold, like a slap in the face. He listed everything he thought was wrong with me: "You're not a nice person anymore. You've let yourself go. You're always angry. You don't look pretty. You've gained weight. I can't live with you like this." His words hit me like daggers, piercing the last fragments of my self-worth.

I moved through each minute, each hour, carrying the unbearable weight of his rejection. But as the days passed, the atmosphere at home grew colder, almost suffocating. His indifference towards me was like a wall I couldn't break through. Slowly, the truth began to sink in—this wasn't just a phase. This was my reality.

Clinging to hope, I turned to his mother for help, praying she might soften his heart or help me understand what to do. Her advice shattered me further: "Just get down on your knees, beg for his forgiveness, and tell him you'll do whatever he wants." I was so desperate that I nearly followed her advice. I stopped short of falling to my knees, but the humiliation was already complete.

Still seeking help, I called his three sisters. Surely, they would understand, I thought. But their responses left me stunned and even more alone. The first was brutally blunt: "He's been putting up with you for many years. Maybe he's just had enough." The second shrugged it off:

"We don't know who's telling the truth—him or you. Sorry, we can't help." The third refused to talk to me at all.

It felt like the walls were closing in. Every door I knocked on slammed shut in my face. Their reactions weren't just indifferent—they felt rehearsed as if they had all been prepared for this moment as if I was the last to know what had been coming for so long. There was no shock, no compassion, no empathy.

My family, on the other hand, rallied around me with unwavering support. My mum, sister, brother-in-law, and cousins called me at least ten times a day, constantly checking in, always hoping to hear that something had changed. They brainstormed ways to save my marriage and even offered to speak to him directly. At first, he refused to engage with them, shutting them out completely. Eventually, I asked my family to stop trying, knowing their futile efforts only added to the tension.

A few weeks later, I decided to take a holiday in India, thinking the distance might clear our minds and give him a chance to realise he didn't want a divorce. Before leaving, I did everything possible to ensure he would miss me. I left the food cupboards bare, the cleaning supplies empty, and there were no pre-cooked meals for him to heat and eat. But as I prepared to go, a painful truth began to dawn on me—I wasn't his partner or lover anymore. I had become his cook, his cleaner, his caretaker. But not a wife or a lover.

In India, I was a wreck. I spent most days sulking and crying, lost in my despair. My family, as always, understood my pain and let me grieve in my way. They tried to cheer me up by playing board games, and though I joined in, my tears never stopped. Every move I made on the board felt heavy with my sadness. Still, I held on to the hope that, somehow, everything would return to how it used to be.

One day, he FaceTimed to speak with our daughter. He didn't ask for me, and I didn't take the lead to talk to him. But as I watched from a distance, something caught my eye—a baby blanket on the sofa behind him. It wasn't ours. My body reacted instantly, a wave of weakness and fever washing over me as if my body knew what my heart refused to accept. Another woman was in his life.

A few days later, he sent me a photo of a beautiful sunset over the woods behind our house. The message read, "I wish you were here." For a fleeting moment, my heart soared. Maybe he missed me after all. But just as quickly, that hope was crushed when the message was instantly deleted shortly after. Deep down, I knew it wasn't meant for me. He had sent it to someone else.

Each night, I went to bed praying this nightmare would end, that I'd wake up and find myself back in our "happy" life. But the denial and despair were consuming me. Despite the growing pile of evidence, I clung to the hope that this was all just a terrible mistake, that the man I once loved would somehow return to me. My mind was trapped in an endless loop of disbelief, refusing to let go of the life I thought we had.

C. BROKEN TRUST, BROKEN HEART

A few weeks later, I returned from India with a heart weighed down by dread and denial, knowing deep inside that nothing had changed. The man I had once loved was still resolute in his decision to end our marriage. As I returned to our home, a strange and suffocating wave of negative energy engulfed me. It was nothing I had ever felt—cold, unwelcoming, and almost accusatory.

The hope I had desperately clung to during my time away began to fracture under the weight of reality. The trust I had fought to keep alive slipped through my fingers, leaving me grasping at nothing. Even the house seemed to scream at me, whispering the presence of another woman, warning me that my instincts weren't wrong.

Little details began to surface as I unpacked and tried to settle back in, each chipping away at my denial. The family photographs that had once adorned the walls were gone, replaced by blank, hollow spaces. In the bathroom, I noticed a box of body products that weren't mine—an intruder's mark left intentionally for me to see. My chest tightened as the realisation crept in: I didn't need any more evidence, but my heart was still fighting the truth.

Unable to process the flood of emotions, I left my daughter with him and drove aimlessly into the night. Tears streamed down my face, blurring my vision as I sobbed uncontrollably. I finally pulled into a quiet spot, parked the car, and called my family. Despite the late hour, they answered, offering comfort and reassurance, staying on the phone until I could catch my breath.

When I returned home, exhausted and emotionally shattered, I found my daughter peacefully asleep in her room. At the same time, he was settled comfortably in the guest room—detached, unbothered, and worlds away from the chaos he had thrown me into.

The following day, fate handed me what my heart had feared but needed to know. His phone, unlocked and unguarded, lay in front of me. Trembling, I picked it up, my curiosity and dread battling within me. What I found was undeniable - her photos, their photos, and messages suggesting seduction and intimacy that he had stolen from me. My stomach churned as if the betrayal was physically poisoning me.

I forced myself to get dressed and drive to work, hoping the routine would ground me, but I couldn't stop crying. By the time I reached the office, I was a wreck, my emotions spiralling out of control. In a moment of panic, I decided to leave my job, take my daughter, and return to India for good.

I called my manager—one of my closest friends—and asked her to meet me outside so I could hand over my laptop. She was already aware of my crumbling personal life and refused to accept my resignation. Instead, she extended my holiday, insisting I take the time to recover. Her compassion became a lifeline I hadn't expected, grounding me in a moment when I felt like I was losing everything.

When I returned home, the confrontation I was trying to avoid happened. I told him I had seen his phone and that there was no use in denying it anymore. The rage I had suppressed erupted. I screamed, the weight of betrayal crushing me. I felt foolish for trusting him, rejected by the man I had built my life around, and utterly broken. Through my tears, I demanded he make a choice: her or me.
He chose her.

Something inside me snapped. In a fit of anger and despair, I stormed out of the house and began knocking on the neighbours' doors, shouting for the world to know the truth—that my husband was a cheater. My voice cracked, and my sobs echoed through the night as he packed his things and left. When the door finally closed behind him, I crumbled to the floor, shaking and crying, my body trembling from the sheer weight of heartbreak.

That night, my anguish followed me into my sleep. I had a vivid, haunting dream that felt more like a vision. In it, he was lying in our bed, tangled with the other woman. Their bodies were entwined, oblivious to my presence as I lay frozen and paralysed, unable to scream or move for fear of touching them. The scene played out like a cruel nightmare, yet it felt so real that when I woke up, my body was drenched in sweat, and my heart pounded in terror.

The dream left me shaken to my core. It wasn't just a product of my imagination—deep down, I knew it was the truth. The bed I had shared with him had been tainted, and the thought of lying in it made my skin crawl. The very next day, I had to get it replaced. It was a small act, but it felt like reclaiming a piece of myself from the wreckage of my shattered trust.

D. DECEIVED AGAIN

Each day after his betrayal was a battle—a desperate attempt to piece together the fragments of a life that no longer felt like mine. My self-worth and self-respect had been shattered into unrecognisable pieces. And yet, despite everything he had done, I longed for him. A part of me still clung to the life we had built, wishing for the comfort of familiarity, the illusion of happiness, and the hope that, somehow, we could go back to what we once were.

I threw myself into survival mode—juggling the responsibilities of a demanding job, caring for my five-year-old daughter, and wrestling with the emotional wreckage of my broken marriage. I read books and articles about mending broken relationships, devouring every piece of advice, whether small or impractical. I tried everything—soft words, hard conversations, even silence—but nothing worked. He was steadfast in his love for her, not me.

Still, I held on to hope. Maybe time would change his heart. Perhaps he would see what he was throwing away. But hope is a cruel master, and before I knew it, three months had passed in this limbo.

Then came Diwali, the festival of light and hope—the victory of good over evil. On that day, I received a phone call that shook me. It was him apologising. He told me he wanted to come back. My heart leapt, not just with hope but with a strange, bitter sense of vindication. The other woman had cheated on him. Karma, I thought. He had been betrayed just as he had betrayed me.

His words stirred a strange mixture of emotions within me—anger, satisfaction, and a tiny, fragile flicker of hope. Despite everything, I was ready to welcome him back. I convinced myself that this was our chance to rebuild, to start fresh. He promised to come home at 7:00 p.m. for the Diwali ritual, and I spent the evening preparing, imagining what it might feel like to have our family whole again.

But, true to form, he was late. When he finally arrived, he offered a cursory apology and acted as if nothing had happened—as if all the pain, betrayal, and heartbreak could be swept under the rug. I suggested couples counselling, hoping he might take this seriously, but his response was cutting: "Why? Do you have a lot of money?"

His dismissiveness felt like a slap in the face. At that moment, it became clear that he hadn't changed. His reasons for returning were not rooted in love or remorse but inconvenience. I needed to hear the truth, so I asked him why he wanted to return.

"I want to be there for our daughter," he said. "I don't want to leave her. I can stay in the guest room."

His words landed like a blow. He didn't want to come back for me. He didn't want to rebuild our marriage or repair the damage. He only wanted to exist in our home for her. What did that even mean? To live as strangers under the same roof? To coexist in the ruins of what we once had?

I took a deep breath, trying to steady my voice, and calmly told him he didn't need to return for our daughter. He could still be in her life without returning to me if she was the only reason. But if he had no desire to be my husband again, there was no point in repairing what was already irreparably broken.

He agreed to take a few days to reflect, saying he would stay with a friend. But as the days passed, he didn't return, and his intentions remained as unclear as ever.

One evening, while discussing the situation with my cousin, suspicion gnawed at us. Something didn't add up. We drove to the other woman's house to see if he had returned to her. It was late, so I had to bring my five-year-old daughter along.

As we turned onto her street, my heart sank. There it was—his car, parked outside her house. He had lied again. He hadn't been with a friend. He had gone straight back to her.

Rage and betrayal coursed through me, a fresh wound atop old scars. I marched up to the house and demanded he come outside. When he did, I slapped him, unable to contain the fury burning inside me. In response, he shoved me, sending me stumbling onto the street. For a moment, time stood still, and every emotion from the past months—hurt, disbelief, rejection, anger—came flooding back in an uncontrollable wave.

When would I learn? Why did I keep trusting him despite the mountain of lies?

My cousin pulled me away, urging me to leave before the situation escalated. We drove back to her house, but he followed us, refusing to let things end there. We spent hours talking, trying to reason with him, but nothing changed.

On the drive home, I was a wreck. The tears came in uncontrollable waves, blinding me as I gripped the steering wheel. My body was shaking, my breath coming in shallow gasps until I had to pull over to vomit. The intensity of my emotions had consumed me entirely.

Through it all, my daughter slept peacefully in the backseat, blissfully unaware of the storm raging in her mother's world. For that small mercy, I was grateful. She didn't deserve to see the chaos or feel the pain that her father and I had inflicted on each other.

E. THE TURNING POINT

Even after being lied to and betrayed countless times, I hadn't reached my breaking point. My stubborn heart refused to let go of the man who hurt me deeply. For months, I clung to the fragile hope that he would come back, that we could somehow rewrite the ending of our shattered story. I told myself that if he could sever all ties with the other woman and truly commit to rebuilding our relationship, maybe—just maybe—we could find our way back to each other.

But I was fighting a lost battle. No amount of reasoning, pleading, or strategising made a difference. I even stooped to blackmail emotionally out of sheer desperation, but nothing worked. Sometimes, I turned the blame inward, agonising over what I could have done differently to save our marriage. I seethed with anger and resentment other times, convinced that the fault lay entirely with him.

The situation was unbearable. Adding salt to the wound, he began to speak openly about his new relationship with me—as if I were some confidant rather than his betrayed wife. Every word felt like a dagger in my heart, breaking me a little more each time. Yet I continued to hold on, hoping against hope that he would wake up and see the truth: that she was only after his money, that what we had was worth saving. I believed—no, I needed to believe—that this nightmare would eventually end.

But then, one cold evening, as I returned from a business trip, my phone buzzed with his text.

"We are expecting."

For a moment, I couldn't breathe. My world tilted on its axis as I stared at the screen, disbelief flooding my veins. Was he serious? How could he have been so reckless? How could he bring another child into this chaos?

This was the same man who had always insisted he valued his freedom and made it clear he didn't want more children. And yet, here he was—about to become a father again with a woman who already had a child from another relationship. It was as if every word he'd ever spoken to me was a lie.

This wasn't just about me anymore. It wasn't just about my daughter. There was now another innocent child entangled in this heartbreaking mess. The weight of that message hit me like a thunderclap.

That message was the tipping point—the moment everything inside me broke. The truth was laid bare, undeniable and unrelenting: this man I had spent years loving and sacrificing for was no longer mine to hold onto. He had gone too far.

A storm of emotions raged within me—anger so fierce it burned through my veins, sadness so deep it felt like drowning, disbelief so sharp it cut me to pieces. I spent sleepless nights in agony, tossing and turning as questions echoed through my mind. How had I ended up here? How could I have let this happen? And, most painfully, why hadn't I let go sooner?

As the days turned into weeks, a painful clarity began to emerge. The man I had loved no longer existed; he had been replaced by someone I didn't recognise, who had broken every vow he'd ever made to me.

The future I had clung to, filled with dreams of love, trust, and family, was an illusion. Slowly, I began to see that waiting for him, hoping for him to change, was like holding onto smoke—futile and self-destructive.

In the quiet moments of solitude, I finally faced the truth: I couldn't keep living in the shadow of a broken dream. It was time to let go of the fantasy I had been clinging to and start building a new reality—for myself, my daughter, and the life we both deserved.

This understanding didn't come in a sudden flash of enlightenment; it crept in gradually, seeping into my heart through countless tears and sleepless nights. Accepting it was agonising, but it was necessary. I could no longer sacrifice my dignity, my peace, or my future for someone who had shown me, time and time again, that I wasn't his priority.

It was over. He wasn't coming back!

Gathering the fragments of my broken heart, I made a choice. I would no longer let his betrayal define me. I would rise from the wreckage, rebuild my life, and reclaim my strength. I would become the woman my daughter could look up to, who showed her that it's never too late to walk away from what no longer serves you.

This wasn't the ending I had envisioned, but it was the beginning of something new—something stronger, something better. And for the first time in months, I felt a glimmer of hope—not for him, but for me.

WHAT I KNOW NOW

1. WORDS MATTER MORE THAN YOU THINK: One of my biggest lessons is never to say something unless you genuinely mean it. During our heated arguments, I quickly said, "Let's break up" or "Maybe we should end this." On two occasions, I even packed my bags, fully expecting him to stop me. Deep down, I knew I wouldn't leave—it was just a desperate cry for attention, a way to make him fight for us.

But the day he turned the tables and suggested divorce, it was like the ground beneath me gave way. When he left, my world shattered into a million pieces. Only then did I understand the weight of those words I had carelessly tossed around.

I couldn't stop replaying every argument in my mind, questioning if I had planted the idea of leaving in his head. Did my empty threats permit him to consider ending it? I was filled with regret, haunted by the realisation that words, once spoken, can take on a life of their own. In my pain, I learned that what we say—especially in moments of anger—can shape our reality in ways we never intended.

2. THEY WILL KEEP BREAKING YOUR HEART UNTIL IT OPENS: Day by day, his actions chipped away at my heart, breaking it into smaller and smaller pieces. Just when I thought the pain had reached its peak, it would find a way to cut deeper. It felt like an endless cycle of heartbreak as if the universe forced me to confront something I wasn't ready to face.

Sometimes, life doesn't just nudge you—it pushes you to your knees, stripping away every layer of denial until you're left raw and exposed. The truth I had been avoiding became impossible to ignore. The pain wasn't just there to hurt me; it was there to awaken me.

It wasn't until I hit rock bottom, crushed by the news of his child with her that my heart finally opened. In that moment of despair, I stopped clinging to what could never be and allowed myself to accept the truth. The heartbreak became a turning point—a painful yet necessary step toward letting go of the past, healing and beginning to rebuild my life.

3. SOMETIMES, THE PERSON YOU'RE TRYING TO SAVE IS YOURSELF: For so long, I thought I was fighting to save him and us. I convinced myself that if I tried harder, loved more profoundly, or endured more, things would change. But the harder I fought, the more I realised I wasn't saving him—I was trying to save myself.

I was trying to save the version of me who believed in love, the woman who thought relationships were built to last no matter what. I was trying to rescue the girl who dreamed of a happy family and the life we had promised each other. In reality, I was fighting for the idea of who I thought I was, not for who I had become.

The breaking point wasn't about losing him but finding me. It was about understanding that I deserved better, that my worth wasn't tied to his choices or love. The journey of healing wasn't just about mending my broken heart—it was about rediscovering my strength and reclaiming the woman I had lost along the way.

9

THE SHIFT IN BALANCE

"We must be willing to let go of the life we've planned,
to have the life that is waiting for us."

— Joseph Campbell.

A. THE BITTER INVASION

Life had taken a harsh and painful turn. I was now living in the aftermath of a separation, facing not only the challenges of dealing with my narcissistic ex-husband but also enduring the presence of his toxic girlfriend, who had forced her way into my reality. This wasn't just about losing a marriage anymore—it felt like my entire life had been overshadowed by bitterness and betrayal.

I got pulled into a competition I never wanted, one where I kept falling short. My ex chose his affair er over me, shattering my confidence and destroying my self-worth. The man I once trusted with my heart made sure to remind me, again and again, how much better he thought she was. He cut deeper with every word and action, making me feel smaller and more broken each day.

Life raged like a cruel, relentless storm. They didn't just try to break me emotionally—they attacked me financially, too. But I refused to surrender. Each time I resisted their control and manipulation, their cruelty intensified. He sent me photos of their intimate moments, flaunting their relationship to deepen my pain. He bombarded me with cruel comparisons, always glorifying her while tearing me down. They constantly called me a bad mum, each word designed to shatter me. And they succeeded. Every image and message stabbed like a dagger into my heart, flooding me with rage, humiliation, and unbearable grief.

In my despair, I lashed out, trying desperately to hurt him the way he had hurt me, but it never brought the relief I craved. The pain lingered, gnawing at me day after day as if I were locked in a losing battle against an unrelenting tide of cruelty. Then, a few months after moving in with her, he demanded to see our daughter more often and insisted on introducing his new girlfriend to her, fueling my already burning heart.

The bitterness I carried deepened when I learned she had been promoted three times within a year—promotions that directly resulted from her affair with her boss, my husband. My focus began to shift away from him and onto her—the woman who had invaded my life without invitation or consent. The word "slut" echoed in my mind, a relentless chant fuelled by anger and disgust. It wasn't just that she had taken my husband; she had bulldozed through the life I had painstakingly built and profited from the wreckage.

My anger toward her consumed me. I saved her number in my phone under the name "Kameeni," a Hindi slang for "bitch," as if that label could somehow dull the edge of my pain. She had destroyed my family, and the fury I felt toward her—and him—was impossible to contain. Being civil to them felt like a cruel, unattainable fantasy.

Every reminder of her—her name, face, and presence in my daughter's life—triggered an uncontrollable storm within me. My chest tightened with rage as I imagined her stepping into roles that were never meant for her, roles that were mine. The helplessness of watching her occupy spaces that once defined my world left me reeling, powerless to stop the cruel march of events.

Night after night, I lay awake, wrestling with unanswerable questions. How could someone like her sleep peacefully, knowing she had stolen another woman's husband, torn apart a family, and walked away without facing any consequences? And what about my husband? How could a man be so cold and cruel, abandoning a decade-long marriage and a five-year-old daughter without remorse, explanation, or support? I couldn't comprehend the injustice of it all. Where was karma? How could someone so selfish and heartless escape accountability and seem to thrive? While I was left grappling with shattered pieces, they moved on with their lives as if the devastation they had caused was inconsequential. My world felt irreparably unfair, a labyrinth of hurt and anger with no clear path out. The weight of that injustice pressed down on me, suffocating me, as I tried to understand why the universe seemed so unforgiving.

B. BATTLING BETRAYAL 2 AGAINST 1

I found myself thrust into an unrelenting battle—a two-against-one struggle for my dignity, my finances, and, most heartbreakingly, my bond with my daughter. It was no longer just about the divorce my ex-husband so desperately pursued. He wanted control over every detail, demanding financial gains even after years of living off my generosity. For nearly a decade, I had supported him, believing in the shared dream of our partnership. But now, my patience had worn thin. I couldn't and wouldn't continue to fund the lifestyle that had torn apart my marriage and my family.

When I stood my ground, his retaliation was merciless. Over and above the emotional drama, he filed for a financial order, confident that his aggression would intimidate me into submission. But instead of caving, I channelled my pain into determination. I prepared myself for the long and gruelling process ahead, ready to invest every ounce of strength and time to ensure the court understood the truth. I had supported him long enough. This fight was about fairness, about standing up for what was right—not just for me, but for the future I envisioned for my daughter.

As the legal battle escalated, so did their cruelty. Their attacks grew more personal and more vindictive, with no line they weren't willing to cross. They called me names, hurled baseless accusations, and threatened to take my daughter away. My ex even dragged social services into the fray, accusing me of being an unfit mother. But what cut deepest was how he used our daughter as a pawn in his game.

He began whispering lies into her innocent ears, twisting her perception of me. They criticised my way of living, demeaned my character, and told her that I had taken all his money. Each word was a dagger aimed at our bond, an attempt to poison her young heart against me. The betrayal wasn't just between him and me anymore; it was now threatening the most sacred relationship—the one between a mother and her child.

Each day felt like an uphill climb with no summit in sight. I spent countless sleepless nights sobbing, my body shaking under the weight of the emotional warfare. It was as if I were drowning in a sea of despair, gasping for air, desperate for relief. The stress, heartache, and fear of losing my daughter consumed me, leaving me raw and exhausted. Yet, even in my darkest moments, my resolve never faltered.

The fear of losing my daughter to their toxic games was a pain far greater than the betrayal itself. I don't know where I found the strength to keep fighting—maybe it came from my deep love for her, or perhaps it was a spark of love for myself, a refusal to endure any more of his cruelty. All I knew was that I couldn't give up. This battle wasn't just about survival; it was about showing her—and reminding myself—that no matter how much they tried to break me, I dared to rise above it all.

WHAT I KNOW NOW

1. 'THE OTHER WOMAN' DID NOT BREAK MY FAMILY: I directed all my anger at his new girlfriend for months, convinced she was the villain who had destroyed my family. I called her names, cursed her existence, and blamed her for every ounce of my pain. In my mind, she was the sole reason my marriage fell apart—the intruder who had stolen the life I had worked so hard to build. But as time passed and the fog of heartbreak began to lift, I faced a truth I couldn't ignore: she wasn't the only one responsible.

Of course, she played a role, but it was my ex who made the choice to betray me, who chose to walk away from our marriage and the life we had built for our daughter. No one forced him to lie, cheat, or leave. Those were his decisions—decisions rooted in his character more than hers. But the hardest truth of all? Our marriage was already on fragile ground long before she appeared. The cracks had been forming for years—unspoken resentments, emotional distance, unresolved conflicts—all building a rift between us. I didn't want to see it then, but we had already begun to drift apart. When she entered the picture, our foundation was so weak that it didn't take much to make it crumble.

Blaming her entirely was a way to shield myself from the pain of facing my role in the relationship's collapse. The reality is that my ex and I both allowed those cracks to grow unchecked. We both made choices—whether through actions or inactions—that contributed to the distance between us.

Pointing fingers at her was more straightforward and less messy. But the truth is far more complicated. No one person destroyed our marriage. It was a slow unravelling, a shared failure to nurture the connection we once had.

2. DIFFICULT TIMES DON'T MAKE A PERSON, THEY REVEAL THEM: It's in the darkest moments that a person's true self emerges. Difficult times strip away the masks people wear, exposing their values, character, and priorities for what they truly are. I lived with a man I thought I knew for nearly a decade. We shared a home, a life, and a child. I believed in him, in us, and in the future we were building together. Yet, when I look back now, I see the red flags I had ignored—apparent signs of his flaws that I excused because I loved him and wanted to hold onto the illusion of our life.

When our relationship fell apart, so did the façade. His true character surfaced, and what I saw was devastating. The man who had once promised to stand by me, to cherish and protect me, became someone I didn't recognise. He didn't just leave me—he shattered me. His actions grew colder, more calculating, as though the years we had spent together were meaningless. He wasn't content to walk away; he seemed determined to erase me, even if it meant causing irreparable harm.

What hurt the most wasn't just his betrayal—it was his complete disregard for our daughter. She was an innocent child caught in the storm, yet he seemed blind to how his actions impacted her. His anger toward me overshadowed his love for her. It was as if her feelings—and mine—were irrelevant in pursuing his selfish desires. He wasn't just indifferent; he was deliberately cruel, seizing every opportunity to wound me further, as though breaking me was his ultimate goal.

Difficult times didn't change him; they unmasked him. The cracks in his character that I had ignored for years became glaring chasms. His lack of empathy, selfishness, and willingness to place his own wants above the well-being of his family—all of it came into sharp, undeniable focus.

And then came the question that haunted me: Did he ever truly love me, or had it all been a lie? The man I thought I knew was gone, leaving only the truth of who he had always been, hidden beneath a mask I so desperately wanted to believe in.

10

ALL ABOUT FINANCES

*"Earning a lot of money is not the key to prosperity.
How to handle it is."*

- unknown

A. FINANCIAL INTELLIGENCE

From the moment we got engaged until the day he left me for another woman, I didn't give my finances the attention they deserved. Growing up, I believed money wasn't worth fighting for. When I saw siblings or relatives bickering over it, I'd quickly judge them, thinking they should just let it go. Culturally, I was raised to see wealth as shared within a marriage—there was no "yours" or "mine," only "ours." I carried this belief into my relationship, never pausing to question if it was mutual. It didn't matter that I had far more to offer financially than he ever did. I loved him, and that was enough—or so I thought.

My upbringing had also left an imprint. Remembering the dowry system, my mum showered him and his family with expensive gifts throughout our marriage. It felt like a way to express gratitude or maintain harmony. I didn't expect anything in return because they never had much to give. Watching my father handle all the financial matters growing up, I unconsciously repeated the pattern in my marriage. I handed over our finances to my husband without a second thought.

Early on, he decided that we didn't need a joint bank account, and I naively trusted his judgment. He claimed I spent too much and suggested we save all the money in his account while using mine for everyday expenses. It sounded reasonable, so I went along with it. When he wanted to send money to his mother in India, he suggested using my Indian account, and I didn't question that either.

Before I knew it, I covered every household expense—mortgage, bills, insurance, shopping, dining out—from my account. When my salary surpassed him, I even set up a direct debit of £500 a month to his account under the guise of saving for "us." I didn't think twice; I believed this was what supportive partners did for each other.

Then came the divorce. When he announced his decision to leave, I was blindsided. His mother called me—not to console me or offer help, but to demand that I return the few pieces of jewellery she had given me. Compared to what my family had given them over the years, her demands were petty, but I returned everything without hesitation. Money and material possessions had never been my priority, and at that time, I believed fighting over them was beneath me.

I let him leave with everything that was his, including the expensive RADO watch I had bought him months before. I never asked for anything back—not even the £500 I had transferred to his account monthly. I thought I was taking the high road.

My illusion that, unlike his family, he was not greedy was shattered during our separation. He took all our valuable possessions and also drained the little savings we had left. He used the savings to fund his new life with her. With what we had worked hard to save, he bought her a brand-new car and other expensive gifts. I had unknowingly financed his affair and paid for the lifestyle he now shared with another woman. It wasn't just the money—it was the betrayal. The man I had trusted with everything had taken advantage of my love and values, turning them into tools for his selfish gain. It felt unbearable, cutting through every ounce of trust I had ever placed in him.

B. THE LEGAL BATTLE

The nightmare didn't end there. When we began discussing the division of finances, his demands became increasingly outrageous, leaving me utterly stunned. Each time I resisted, his requests grew more brazen and audacious.

He insisted I sell the family home and hand over 50% of the proceeds—my sanctuary, the one place that still felt like a haven. The very thought of losing it was terrifying. Worse, he refused to contribute a single penny toward our daughter's expenses or the upkeep of the home—a property whose value had increased solely because of my payments. His demands reached absurd levels when he escalated matters by sending me a legal notice. He wanted half of the house, half of my business value, and whatever remaining assets I had. He was asking for sums I didn't even have.

The imbalance in our financial transparency stared me in the face. I had handed over every detail of my finances to him, yet I knew almost nothing about his. It became clear he had likely hidden assets, shielding them from me while exploiting the legal system to extract as much as possible.

Every conversation, every document, and every interaction that followed became a dreaded ordeal. I spent countless weekends in spreadsheets, sifting through old records to untangle the mess. With every form I filled out, the weight of my past choices bore down on me. I had trusted him unquestioningly, ignoring every red flag of his greed. The painful realisation hit me: I had been nothing more than an ATM to him—the real reason he married me. He never let me leave my job, not because he cared about my career but because he depended on my income to sustain our lifestyle. While I entered the marriage out of insecurity, he did so out of greed.

This bitter truth left me feeling foolish. I vowed I wouldn't let a single extra penny go to him if I could help it. It was no longer about the money but about reclaiming my dignity and standing firm on my principles.

The legal battle dragged on for nearly four years, slowed by the process and his constant deceit. He lied repeatedly, missed deadlines, and manipulated the system. Since it was a family law case and not a criminal one, he faced no real consequences for his actions. Adding to the betrayal, he secretly en-cashed fixed deposits and insurance policies in our daughter's name, robbing her of the financial security I had carefully planned for her future.

The most heartbreaking part was his manipulation of our daughter. Despite being on the winning end of the settlement, he told her blatant lies—that I had taken all his money and left him destitute. It was crushing to see him use her as a pawn, trying to turn her against me with his fabrications.

WHAT I KNOW NOW

1. FINANCIAL COMPATIBILITY IS A CORNERSTONE OF A HEALTHY RELATIONSHIP

Financial compatibility is not just about sharing expenses or having joint accounts—it's about aligning values, priorities, and attitudes toward money. Partners holding fundamentally different views on finances can create deep and lasting conflicts that extend far beyond the numbers. In my case, the disparity was stark. He operated from a place of scarcity, perpetually consumed by the fear of not having enough, while I embraced an abundance mindset, trusting in growth, prosperity, and the future.

This difference represented our opposing worldviews when it came to money. For him, money was a finite resource to be hoarded and controlled, driven by anxiety and insecurity. For me, money was a tool to create opportunities, invest in the future, and build a better life. These clashing beliefs made it nearly impossible to find common ground—whether about saving, spending, investing, or planning for the future. What started as minor disagreements about financial decisions eventually became a recurring source of tension.

To maintain peace and avoid constant arguments, I made the mistake of entirely relinquishing control of our finances to him. At the time, it was a practical solution accepted by society. However, over time, it led to growing resentment on my part. His restrictive, fear-driven approach felt stifling and dismissive of my vision for the future. On the other hand, my willingness to defer to him likely fed into his need for control, creating a power imbalance that further strained our relationship.

Financial compatibility isn't just about avoiding conflict—it's about building trust and creating a shared vision for your life together. When one partner shoulders all the financial responsibility, it can breed resentment, erode respect, and undermine the partnership. I learned this lesson the hard way. Our inability to communicate and align on financial goals became a silent wedge, slowly driving us apart.

2. FINANCIAL INDEPENDENCE IS ESSENTIAL FOR A WOMAN: Financial independence is more than a practical necessity—it is a foundation for self-respect, freedom, and resilience. It's not simply about earning money; it's about having the power to make decisions about your life, choices, and future without relying on anyone else.

Although I had handed over control of our finances to my ex-husband, my saving grace was that I was not financially dependent on him. I could support myself and my daughter, and that independence gave me the strength to face the following upheaval. It allowed me to stand firm and make decisions in our best interests, even when the road ahead was fraught with challenges.

Unfortunately, I've spoken to many women who are not in the same position. Their financial dependence on their spouses traps them in toxic relationships, making it nearly impossible for them to leave. Fear of financial instability often forces them to endure unhealthy dynamics for far too long—sometimes for their entire lives. This lack of independence becomes a silent prison, eroding their confidence, self-worth, and ability to envision a better future.

True financial independence goes beyond earning an income; it means being equipped to navigate life on your terms. It means understanding your finances, building savings, and making informed choices about managing your money. It is a shield against uncertainty, offering security when the unexpected happens and a pathway to reclaiming your power in the face of adversity.

Financial independence also fosters emotional autonomy. When you're not reliant on someone else to meet your basic needs, you're free to set boundaries, demand respect, and walk away from relationships that no longer serve you. It is the ultimate form of self-care, ensuring your worth isn't tied to anyone else's actions or decisions.

If I could offer one piece of advice to every woman, this: start today. No matter your circumstances, take steps to secure your financial independence. Invest in your education, build skills, save where you can, and take control of your financial future. It's not just about surviving—it's about thriving with the confidence to create the life you deserve.

3. IT IS NOT WRONG TO FIGHT FOR YOUR RIGHTS: For years, I believed that fighting over things like money, property, or possessions was beneath me. I told myself, *If someone takes from you, let them have it. Material things don't matter.* But when my marriage ended, I was forced to confront a hard truth: this wasn't just about money or material possessions. It was about standing up for myself, my worth, and my future.

If I didn't fight for what I had earned—what was rightfully mine—how could I expect anyone else to respect me? Letting go without a fight would have meant accepting the narrative they tried to write for me: that I didn't matter or deserve a voice or a share in the life I had helped build.

This wasn't just a financial battle but a battle for my dignity, boundaries, and self-respect. My ex-husband and his new partner weren't content with what they had already taken. They wanted more. They wanted my home, tried to manipulate my daughter, and sought to erode my self-worth piece by piece. They pushed and demanded as if their goal was to erase me from my own life, leaving nothing of the woman I once was.

By standing up for myself, I wasn't just protecting my rights but reclaiming my power. I showed my daughter that we don't have to accept less than we deserve and that standing up for ourselves is not selfish but necessary. In fighting for what was mine, I was also fighting for her, teaching her that her worth isn't negotiable and that boundaries are worth defending.

This fight was exhausting and emotionally draining, and every time I felt like giving up, I reminded myself that this wasn't just about a house or money. It wasn't about revenge or greed—it was about respect. It was about saying, *"I matter. My contributions matter. My voice matters.»*

11

THROUGH THE PAIN, TOWARDS FORGIVENESS AND FREEDOM

"If you never heal from what hurt you, you will bleed on people who didn't cut you"

A. LEANING INTO THE STORM, FEELING THE PAIN

The legal battle felt never-ending, an exhausting routine of signing papers, meeting deadlines, and constantly dealing with him. It was overwhelming, leaving me with little time to breathe. But even with all the chaos surrounding me, I knew I had to find ways to heal. If I didn't care for myself, the weight of it all would crush me.

I was stuck in a loop of confusion and hurt, with regret whispering cruel "what ifs" in my mind. Happy memories would replay like scenes from an old movie, leaving me wishing I could go back and rewrite the story. Then there was the anger—hot, fierce, and all-consuming. It made me want to confront him, to unload the rage I had carried in silence for so long. It was a storm of endless emotions, knocking me down every time I tried to stand.

But I had been handling the pain all wrong. I kept pushing it away, pretending it didn't exist or burying it under distractions. But the more I ignored it, the louder it became, demanding my attention like a child throwing a tantrum. Eventually, I came to understand that I couldn't run from it. The only way forward was to face the pain, lean into it, and allow myself to feel it truly—no matter how scary that seemed. I had to permit myself to sit with the hurt, to be vulnerable, and to take the time I needed to heal. No pushing, no judging, no blaming—just allowing myself to be present with it, however messy it felt.

It wasn't easy. Sitting with my pain felt like standing at the edge of a dam, unsure of what would happen when the floodgates opened. But I started with small steps. Guided meditations often left me in tears, but I stayed with them. Journaling became my outlet, my pen trembling as I poured out feelings I couldn't express. Walks in nature became moments of quiet connection, where I cried, yelled, or let my pain have a voice. Slowly, the storm began to calm, even if only a little at first.

Leaning into the hurt didn't erase it, but it changed how it lived within me. Its grip started to loosen, and I began to reclaim pieces of myself.

I've learned to accept that some pain doesn't entirely disappear—and that's okay. It's no longer a roaring presence but a quiet reminder of where I've been and how far I've come. Nine years have passed since I heard those shattering words, "I want a divorce." The pain still surfaces occasionally, like a faint scar, but it no longer defines me.

B. FORGIVENESS: THE FIRST STEP TO LETTING GO OF VICTIMHOOD

Although I was starting to acknowledge my pain a lot more, my identity had morphed into the woman who had been betrayed, the one who had suffered adultery. Whenever I introduced myself, I mentioned that I was a single mom. It became my badge, something I wore to let people know I had endured hardship. In my mind, it justified my anger and made me more deserving of sympathy. But in reality, it was holding me back.

I blamed him for destroying our family. It felt righteous to do so. He was the villain; I was the victim. This narrative comforted me in my pain but also kept me stuck. It was easier to stay angry at him than to look within and confront the deeper truths of my situation.

But I also knew this: if I wanted to free myself, I had to stop clinging to the pain. I couldn't let his actions define me any longer. I had to take control of my life and let go of the victimhood; I had to start by forgiving him, forgiving him to break free from the chains of anger and reclaiming my life.

Ironically, my name—Kshama—means "forgiveness." My entire life, I carried a name that symbolised grace and letting go. And yet, in this moment, forgiveness felt impossible. How could I forgive someone who wasn't even sorry? Someone who, in his ego and arrogance, likely never thought twice about the damage he caused? Forgiveness felt like a betrayal—like I was excusing his behaviour, letting him off the hook, and giving up my right to feel hurt.

My coach became my guide on this challenging journey. She gave me a simple task that felt impossible—saying one good thing about him daily. It felt absurd. How could I say anything good about someone who had shattered my trust? Each attempt felt fake, forced, and insincere. My anger was too raw, my pain too overwhelming.

So, I began practising forgiveness meditations. But every time I tried, my mind returned to the same place—his betrayal. I would sit silently, yet my thoughts screamed with accusations: *He destroyed everything. He ruined us.* Writing in my journal was no better. I filled the pages angrily, using harsh words to describe him and her. It became a way to keep the pain at bay, to shield myself from the deeper hurt I wasn't ready to face.

The meditations, the journaling, the raw honesty—they slowly began to shift something within me. Day after day, I allowed myself to feel the full weight of my emotions. I cried until I thought I couldn't cry anymore.

Then, little by little, the weight started to lift. It wasn't dramatic or sudden; it was gradual, like a tightly wound rope loosening bit by bit. My shoulders felt lighter, my heart less burdened. I wasn't just shedding the anger—I was letting go of the need for an apology, the need to hear him say, "I'm sorry."

Forgiveness became something much more profound than I'd ever imagined. It wasn't about excusing what he did or pretending it didn't hurt. It was about releasing myself from the power his actions had over me. It was about acknowledging that I might never get closure from him and deciding that I didn't need it to move forward.

In one guided meditation, I pictured him in my mind. I visualised cutting the chains that tied me to him—the anger, the blame, the endless cycle of resentment. Tears poured down my face as I imagined the chains falling away, and for the first time, I felt the faintest sense of freedom.

There's no denying the journey was painful. There were days when the anger came rushing back, and I let it sit for a while. But now, I knew I had the tools to move on. Forgiveness wasn't a one-time event; it was a practice, a daily commitment to myself.

Forgiving him, without the apology I longed for, was the ultimate act of self-love. It wasn't about forgetting what he did or minimising its impact. It was about choosing peace for myself, even when he wasn't sorry.

With every step, I moved closer to healing. I began to see that forgiveness wasn't just in my name—it was in my power. In choosing to forgive, I was reclaiming the life I deserved.

C. WHAT I KNOW NOW

1. YOU CAN BE RIGHT, OR YOU CAN BE HAPPY: I held tightly to the belief that I was right for a long time. I had been wronged, betrayed, and hurt, and my anger felt justified—and it was. But no matter how right I thought I was, it didn't bring me peace. It didn't

Heal the ache in my heart or change anything about my life.

He wasn't coming back, and there was no prize for enduring the pain. The hardest truth to face was that my daughter wasn't benefiting from my stubborn righteousness. If anything, she was absorbing my bitterness and anger, even though she didn't understand the reasons behind them.

At some point, I had to ask myself the tricky question: "What do I want?" The answer was simple but profound: I wanted peace. I wanted to be happy again. For that to happen, I had to let go of the need to be correct. I could continue to be right and miserable or let go of my need to be correct and happy.

Don't get me wrong—my righteousness still shows up occasionally, especially when he does something thoughtless or hurtful again. For a while, I let it simmer. I replay the old narratives in my mind and feel the anger rise. But now, I recognise it for what it is—a temporary distraction, a tug back to a version of myself I no longer want to be.

When those moments come, I remind myself that holding on to being right comes at the cost of my peace and happiness. And nothing, not even my pride, is worth that. So, I make the conscious choice to release it, not because it's easy, but because it's necessary for me—and for the life I want to create for myself and my daughter.

2. FORGIVE OTHERS FOR YOURSELF, NOT FOR THEM: This was one of the hardest truths I had to face. I used to believe that forgiveness meant excusing his actions or letting him off the hook. But that's not what forgiveness is about. Forgiveness isn't for the person who hurt you—it's for you, for yourself, and for your own peace.

After everything he did, it was clear he probably wasn't even thinking about me. He didn't care about the pain he caused. And even if, deep down, he knew he was wrong, his ego would never let him admit it. I was stuck while he was moving on with his life and building a new relationship with his partner. I replayed the betrayal in my mind like a broken record, letting it consume me. My resentment wasn't affecting him—it was only hurting me.

As I started to forgive him, I understood that forgiveness didn't mean saying his actions were acceptable or pretending they hadn't caused damage. Forgiveness meant freeing myself from the emotional prison I had built. It meant releasing the grip of anger and blame that was holding me back.

As Mark Twain wisely said, *"Forgiveness is the fragrance the violet sheds on the heel that has crushed it."* Forgiveness is not a weakness; it is a strength. It is a choice to stop allowing someone else's actions to control my emotions and my life. By forgiving, I wasn't letting him off the hook—I was setting myself free.

3. HEALING IS NOT LINEAR: Healing is a journey, and it's far from neat or predictable. It's messy, complicated, and sometimes downright overwhelming. It's not a smooth road where every step feels like progress or success. Instead, it's full of twists and turns, moments of clarity that make you feel on top of the world, and then days that leave you questioning everything, feeling like you're back where you started.

I've had moments where I felt unstoppable, where hope lit up even the darkest corners of my heart. But I've also had days when the weight of it all felt unbearable, days when moving forward seemed impossible. And you know what? That's okay.

Healing has taught me that setbacks don't erase the steps I've taken. Falling doesn't mean I've failed. It means I'm human. It's not about arriving at some perfect, pain-free version of life. It's about learning to live fully—embracing the highs and the lows, finding beauty in the mess, and cultivating resilience even when the ground beneath me feels unsteady.

I've understood that healing is less about "fixing" and more about accepting. Accept that life is imperfect, that I am imperfect, and that growth often comes from the very struggles I wish I could avoid. It's about showing myself grace on the hard days and celebrating the small victories, even when they feel insignificant.

Healing isn't a straight path—it's a journey of learning, unlearning, and becoming. And every step is still progress, no matter how small or shaky.

12

FROM HEARTBREAK TO SELF-DISCOVERY

*"Until you make peace with who you are,
you will never be content with what you have"*

A. A NEW PURPOSE

As I worked on forgiving and taking back control of my life, I also did a lot of soul-searching. The legal battles and their cruelty were relentless, but facing the truth about my choices was the most challenging. How naive I had been. I had believed so many lies, given my love so freely, and sacrificed years of my life for someone who didn't value me.

The pain wasn't just from losing him—it was from seeing how many red flags I had ignored to keep the illusion of happiness alive. When I finally faced the reality of my situation, I felt utterly lost.

A terrifying reality emerged: I had no direction, goal, or vision for the future. My dreams were in ruins, and I was left in the wreckage, unsure of where to go or who I was. If I wasn't waiting for him anymore, then what? Where did that leave me?

My confidence had been eroded to the point where rebuilding my life felt insurmountable. The label of "single mother" hung over me like a storm cloud, a constant reminder of the stigma and judgment I feared. Though my career appeared successful on the surface, it was a hollow facade, hiding the pain and emptiness that gnawed at my soul. Every day, I went through the motions—showing up for work, managing the basics—but inside, I was drowning.

As days turned into weeks, I was consumed by frustration, sorrow, and an overwhelming sense of failure. When my birthday came, I made a simple, almost desperate resolution: I wouldn't cry over him anymore. I decided to cook a meal for myself—something just for me. As I stood in the kitchen, staring blankly at the ingredients, I was struck by an unsettling realisation: *I didn't even know what I liked to eat anymore.* I had spent so many years catering to someone else's preferences, living a life shaped around his needs and desires, that I had lost touch with myself.

That moment hit me harder than any legal battle or insult ever could. It was a stark, devastating revelation: *I no longer knew who I was.* I couldn't remember the last time I did something purely for my joy and fulfilment. *I had become a stranger to myself. I had lost myself!*

Another truth surfaced: *I did not respect myself. I did not love myself.* How could I expect him—or anyone else—to value me when I had failed to value myself? The weight of this reality broke me. I collapsed onto the floor, sobbing uncontrollably for all the years I had spent neglecting my worth, for the version of myself I had abandoned in the name of love and compromise.

In that moment of despair, I stood at a crossroads, faced with a choice: I could let this heartbreak consume me, define my story, and dictate the rest of my life, or I could use it as a turning point to rise above the pain and rediscover who I indeed was. That day, I chose *to rise above, reclaim my strength, and find the person I had lost along the way.*

I chose to be a better role model for my daughter. She deserved a mother who could show her what strength looked like and teach her the value of self-respect and resilience. My daughter became my reason to push forward.

B. RECLAIMING MY IDENTITY

That day, *I chose —to rise above, to reclaim my strength, and to find the person I had lost along the way.*

But despite being a strong, independent woman, marriage had subtly transformed me into a reflection of the role models I grew up with—my mother, sister, and aunts. Unknowingly, I had mirrored what I had seen as a child, slipping into unhealthy patterns I hadn't even realised I was repeating.

Yet, amidst the devastation, one unexpected gift was my relationship with my mother. Ours were always strained, marked by conflict, differing opinions, and emotional distance. For most of my life, we were at odds, clashing over everything from big decisions to minor details. But during this turbulent phase, our relationship took a complete turn. The woman I never imagined would be my ally became my most substantial support.

We started talking every day. Once laced with judgment and tension, our conversations grew softer, warmer, and more genuine. For the first time, I felt a sense of comfort in her words, a balm for my wounded heart. Then, one day, during one of our chats, she said something that stopped me in my tracks:

"You know, the old Kshama—the one who stayed back in Mumbai and fought with me and always did what she believed in—I miss her. I want her back."

Her words hit me like a lightning bolt. She had already sensed what I was only beginning to understand—that I had lost myself. Whether intentional or not, her words gently guided me back to who I once was.

Her voice echoed in my mind long after our call ended. I couldn't stop replaying her words. I had been so consumed by my struggles that I hadn't noticed how far I had strayed from the spirited, confident woman I used to be.

I began reflecting deeply. Who was I back then? What made me, *me*, before life stripped away my essence? Memories started to surface—the small joys, the fierce determination, the unapologetic self-belief that had once defined me. I remembered how I had fought to stay in Mumbai against my mother's wishes, relying on nothing but my inner wisdom and courage. I recalled staying above petty gossip and drama, pouring my energy into building my life, brick by brick, on my terms.

The memories stirred something powerful in me. I didn't want to survive this heartbreak—I wanted to reclaim myself. So, I took action. I started with small but significant steps. I made a list of everything that used to light me up, and at the top was taking care of my body. My body had always been my source of insecurity, but looking after myself had also been a source of strength and confidence for me.

Without hesitation, I signed up for a program with a celebrity nutritionist. It was expensive, but for the first time in years, I didn't feel guilty about investing in myself. I also invested in a fitness club with everything I needed—a gym, swimming pool, and sauna. It became my sanctuary, where I could heal physically and emotionally. Every workout, every swim, every quiet moment in the sauna felt like a small victory, a step closer to finding myself again.

But it wasn't just about my body. I knew I needed to heal my mind and soul too. I signed up for courses and workshops that reignited my passions and pushed me to grow. One of my most transformative decisions was enrolling in *life coaching with Anna Garcia.* In those sessions, I confronted my deepest traumas, peeling back the layers of pain and uncovering the resilience I had buried for so long.

With every step, I felt lighter. The weight of the past, the years of betrayal and heartbreak, began to lift. I started to smile more often—not the polite smile you wear for others, but a genuine smile from within. I laughed more. I even began to look younger, as though reclaiming my identity was rejuvenating me from the inside out.

I also poured my energy into my relationship with my daughter. We spent more time together, making up silly songs, dancing around the house, and laughing until our sides hurt. We started travelling across Europe, creating memories that would last a lifetime. Each trip brought us closer, and with every shared experience, I felt a sense of pride. I was giving her the best of me—not just material comforts but a mother who was present, joyful, and strong.

For the first time in years, I felt alive. I wasn't just existing; I was living. Reclaiming my identity wasn't easy—it took time, effort, and a lot of courage. But it was worth every moment. Piece by piece, I was rebuilding myself. I wasn't just becoming the Kshama my mother had longed to see again—I was becoming the Kshama I needed to be—for myself, for my daughter, for the life I deserved.

C. EMBRACING SOLITUDE AND CULTIVATING INNER STRENGTH

As I continued my journey, I started finding comfort in my company. I was no longer afraid to be alone. For the first time, solitude wasn't something to fear but rather to cherish. I embraced it wholeheartedly, allowing it to become my sanctuary.

Many of my friends and family couldn't understand my path. They weren't walking the same journey, so our connections began to feel hollow. I stopped enjoying the silly gatherings where people talked endlessly about who did what or said what. Gossip lost its allure, replaced by a growing disinterest in trivial matters. My focus turned inward, and I found peace in simply being with myself.

Being alone gave me the time and bandwidth to reflect—deeply. I began to confront and heal not only from my divorce but also from the scars of my childhood traumas. There were wounds I had buried so deep that I'd forgotten they existed. Solitude gave me the space to acknowledge them, to sit with my pain, and to begin letting it go.

With the time I saved from being anti-social, I began cultivating new habits that nourished my mind, body, and soul. My mornings started with meditation—a practice that became the anchor of my day. Sitting quietly with my thoughts, focusing on my breath, I found a sense of clarity and calm I had never experienced before. In the evenings, I turned to journaling. Putting pen to paper allowed me to untangle the knots in my mind and release emotions I didn't even know I was holding onto.

I looked forward to my gym sessions, which became more than just a workout; they were a testament to my commitment to myself. Over the weekends, I replaced the mindless drama of TV shows with something far more enriching: self-help videos and courses. I immersed myself in this world of growth, hungry for knowledge and eager to evolve.

During this time, I discovered Audible, and it became a companion in my solitude. On average, I listened to two books a month, absorbing their wisdom as I went about my day. While many books left an impact, two stood out as transformative for me back then: *Conversations with God* by Neale Donald Walsch and *Change Your Thoughts, Change Your Life* by Wayne Dyer. These books reshaped how I thought about life, purpose, and power. They gave me new perspectives, teaching me that life wasn't happening to me but for me.

For three to four years, I remained in this sacred growth space. It was a time of immense transformation, where every day felt like a step closer to becoming the person I was meant to be. As my self-care deepened, so did my love for myself. I began to see myself in a new light, no longer defined by past failures or betrayals. I started to rebuild my confidence, piece by piece. The more I nurtured myself, the more I was able to show up fully in my life. I became a more present and joyful mother, a more supportive and happier friend, and a confident, capable team player at work.

The solitude I once dreaded became my comfort zone. It taught me more about myself and gave me answers to questions I never thought I'd find. Why had my life played out the way it had? What was my purpose? Slowly but surely, I started to see the bigger picture of life.

The past storms became the bedrock of my resilience—a testament to how far I had come and a promise of how much further I could go. As I write this chapter, I feel a steady surge of strength, a fire of motivation urging me forward. It's a quiet but powerful reminder to keep striving, evolving, and embracing every opportunity to become a better version of myself.

WHAT I KNOW NOW

1. THE MOST IMPORTANT RELATIONSHIP IS THE ONE YOU HAVE WITH YOURSELF: The most important relationship you will ever have is the one you have with yourself. Every other relationship in your life is a reflection of that. It took me years to understand this, but now I see how true it is.

For as long as I can remember, my mum told me I wasn't supporting her. She brought this up often, and it left me feeling guilty and inadequate. Then, after I got married, I heard the same complaint from my husband. It was as if the universe had hit "repeat."

At first, I thought it was just bad luck—I was surrounded by people who didn't see how hard I was trying. But as I began working on my self-awareness, the pattern became clear. *Truth be told, the one person I wasn't supporting wasn't my mum or my husband—it was me.*

I had spent so much of my life putting others' needs first, trying to meet their expectations, and chasing external validation that I had completely neglected myself. I wasn't listening to my needs or standing up for what I wanted. And in their ways, my mum and my husband held up a mirror, showing me what I had been refusing to see.

I began to ask myself the questions I had avoided for so long: *What do I need? What does support look like for me?* Slowly, I started showing up for myself, setting boundaries, and giving myself the love and care I had always sought in others.

The most incredible thing happened when I did this. My relationships with others began to shift. I stopped needing their validation as I learned to nurture and support myself. I became less reactive, more understanding, and more at peace.

What I know now is that how others treat us often mirrors how we treat ourselves. When we neglect ourselves, it shows up in our relationships. But when we start prioritising the relationship with ourselves, everything changes. Life becomes less about fixing others and more about healing within. And that healing? It ripples outward, transforming how we see and connect with the world.

2. AUTHENTICITY IS THE FOUNDATION OF A LASTING RE-LATIONSHIP: For any relationship to thrive, both people must show up as their authentic selves. Pretending to be someone you're not might create the illusion of harmony for a while, but it's like building a house on unstable ground—it can't hold forever. The cracks will show, and eventually, the whole structure will crumble.

When you hide your true self, you're living a lie, and lies can grow. They create distance, resentment, and frustration as the gap between who you are and who you pretend to be becomes impossible to ignore.

Sooner or later, the real you will surface—often in anger, exhaustion, or bitterness—causing damage that could have been avoided.

My relentless pursuit of perfection slowly eroded who I was in my marriage. I tried so hard to meet expectations—his, society's, and even my own—that I became someone I didn't recognise. At first, I convinced myself it was necessary to keep the peace and maintain the image of a perfect partner. But over time, the facade became too heavy to bear, and I started to break under its weight.

Lasting love isn't built on illusions or perfection. It's built on honesty, vulnerability, and a willingness to accept and embrace each other's flaws. Real love happens when both people are brave enough to show up fully, with all their imperfections, and still choose each other every single day.

Authenticity isn't just the foundation of a lasting relationship; it allows love to grow, deepen, and endure. Only when you're true to yourself can you build a safe, meaningful, and unshakeable connection.

3. THE UNIVERSE IS ALWAYS SPEAKING—YOU NEED TO LISTEN: As I walked through this journey, I stumbled upon a truth that changed everything: the universe always speaks to us. It doesn't announce itself loudly or present answers wrapped in neon signs. Instead, it speaks softly through subtle moments and quiet messages we often dismiss.

Sometimes, my mother reminded me to reconnect with the person I once was, urging me to remember my strength. Other times, it came through the words of a book I was reading or listening to—words that seemed to hold just the needed answers. A passing comment from a stranger, or even a phrase scribbled on a wall, would suddenly feel deeply personal, as though it was meant just for me.

But the most profound conversations were the ones I had with myself. We often carry the answers we seek—we need to listen. Have you ever flipped a coin to make a decision and realised, before it even lands, that your heart already knows the choice you truly want? That's your intuition speaking, your inner wisdom guiding you.

During meditation or reflection, I would sit with my questions in quiet moments, and the answers would come clear and instant. These

FROM HEARTBREAK TO SELF-DISCOVERY | 119

weren't ideas I invented or forced into being. They were my deeper knowing, my intuition showing me the way. Through my heart, it was as if the universe was pointing me toward clarity.

When you carry a question in your heart, the universe finds ways to guide you toward the answer. It whispers through people, moments, and signs, but most importantly, it speaks through your inner voice. You must quiet the noise around you to hear it, trust yourself, and truly listen. The answers are there—they've always been—waiting for you to notice them.

4. BEING ALONE DOESN'T MEAN BEING LONELY: Many people confuse solitude with loneliness, but they are not the same. Loneliness is a sense of emptiness, a yearning for connection that feels out of reach. Solitude, on the other hand, is a sacred space—a place where you can retreat, reflect, and reconnect with yourself.

In the stillness of being alone, I found room to think deeply and heal from the wounds of my past. It was in these quiet moments that I began to understand myself truly. Solitude became my sanctuary, offering me the clarity and strength to let go of old pain and rebuild my inner world.

But solitude didn't just give me space; it also revealed who I was at my core. I began to notice the small things—what I liked to eat, the kind of shows or books that spoke to me, how I preferred to spend my evenings, and what brought me joy. I discovered who I was when no one else's preferences or expectations shaped my choices. For the first time in years, I understood myself as an individual, separate from any relationship or role.

This understanding was transformative. The more I learned about myself, the more I realised how important it is to show up authentically in relationships. By trying always to please the other, I was eroding my authenticity. You can only bring your true self to others when you know and accept who you are.

Through this journey, I discovered how fulfilling it is to enjoy my company. I didn't need anyone else to fill a void or make me feel complete. Being alone wasn't something to fear; it was a chance to grow, connect with myself, and find strength in my presence.

Solitude taught me that being alone is not a burden but a gift—a powerful opportunity to deepen one's connection with oneself and build a life rooted in authenticity and inner harmony.

13

NAVIGATING LIFE WITH A NARCISSISTIC EX

"Everything you say can and will be used against you"

A. UNDERSTANDING WHO I AM DEALING WITH

While I was working on myself—rebuilding my confidence, rediscovering my purpose, and healing from the wounds of the past—my ex's antics continued unabated. His behaviour seemed deliberately designed to disrupt my progress, as though he thrived on keeping me entangled in his chaos. Every interaction felt like a calculated move to create conflict, and his actions sent a clear message: *"If I'm not happy, you won't be either,"* or worse, *"If I don't have money, I'll make sure you don't either."* These were not just empty threats; they manifested in his refusal to provide financial support, constant attempts to drag me into arguments, and a relentless effort to undermine my peace. Our legal battle dragged on for four excruciating years when I learned much about myself and began to see him for who he truly was.

For the longest time, whilst being married, I struggled to understand why our interactions were so draining, so toxic. There was a coldness, an emotional void that felt impossible to bridge. But as I dove deeper into self-awareness, therapy, and research, the puzzle pieces began to fit together. I was dealing with a narcissist. Narcissists thrive on control, manipulation, and the ability to keep others off balance. They use tactics like gaslighting, where they distort reality so effectively that you start doubting your sanity. They crave attention and validation and will go to any lengths to keep the spotlight on themselves—even if it means sowing chaos and pain in others' lives. For him, it is always about maintaining control and ensuring that I remain as miserable and disoriented as he was.

Looking back, the signs had been there all along, even during our marriage. He controlled every aspect of our finances, deciding where I could work, how much I could spend, and even where we spent our holidays. My ex ignored all my good qualities but highlighted all my vices. I never received a 'thank you' or 'well done' or 'I am proud of you', but I always heard words like 'If they are saying then maybe you need to work on yourself' or 'I think you need to change the way you communicate at work'. He would scrutinise and criticise me, pointing out every perceived flaw when I felt low. Instead of building me up, he capitalised on my insecurities, reinforcing them until I believed I was unworthy. He projected his fears and failures onto me, painting a narrative where I was always at fault. After our separation, his attacks became more personal. He called me a bad mother, accusing me of neglecting our daughter, even as he prioritised his girlfriend over his parental responsibilities. But as I began to see through his patterns, I realised these accusations weren't rooted in truth—they were projections of his guilt and insecurities.

B. CO-PARENTING WITH A NARCISSISTIC EX

When your ex is a narcissist, co-parenting doesn't exist. What you're doing is navigating a battlefield. Every interaction feels like a potential conflict, and the struggle seems endless.

He would agree on a pick-up time for our daughter but show up an hour late. When he arrived, he would draw attention, honking endlessly and making a scene in front of the neighbours. When I raised the issue, it led to days of relentless arguing. Even to this day, my daughter is 14 but traumatised about the pick-ups. Just in case, she gets ready half an hour before the pick-up time.

In addition, even agreeing on holidays was a nightmare. Whenever he wanted to move things around, he would do so without hesitation, but whenever I needed help with childcare, he would flatly refuse. His actions were always self-serving, and I was left to shoulder the burden.

No matter how neutral or reasonable I tried to be, he always found a way to escalate things. Conversations about our daughter's well-being quickly turned into a tug-of-war. Every point I made would get twisted, and he'd throw in unrelated issues, creating so much confusion that I would lose track of what we discussed. It drained me emotionally. I would cry and vent to my mom after every interaction. It felt never-ending.

I reached a point where I couldn't take the constant arguing anymore. I just wanted it to stop. I repeatedly told my mom, "I just want to shut up with him." So, I made it my mission to break that cycle. Day after day, month after month, I worked hard to stop engaging with him. It wasn't easy. A part of me always wanted to have the last word, defend myself, and ensure I was heard. But with a narcissist, there is no winning. *The only way to win is to refuse to play the game at all.*

C. MASTERING THE ART OF DETACHMENT AND SETTING BOUNDARIES

In time, I learned to stop reacting. I trained myself to stay calm and distant, no matter how much he provoked me. The most effective way was to detach from his chaos emotionally. My ex thrived on creating drama, constantly stirring up conflict. But I did not have to participate in his games. His goal was to confuse and control, but I found strength in simplicity: stick to the point, stay grounded, and don't let him pull me into his web of drama.

Setting boundaries with him became essential for my survival. One of the first and most crucial boundaries I set was moving all communication to email. Phone calls were too volatile, and they always left me emotionally drained and confused. With email, I could take my time to process his words and respond only to what was truly necessary. I stopped engaging with his insults, provocations, and efforts to derail the conversation. Instead, I focused solely on what mattered: the decisions regarding our daughter.

Along with this, I began setting clear rules for myself. If I felt emotionally triggered or overwhelmed, I refused to engage. I allowed myself to step back, take a deep breath, and respond only when calm. *Over time, I shifted from asking him how things should be to telling him how they would be.* I stated the schedule instead of requesting his agreement on visitation times. This shift gave me a sense of control and minimised the opportunities for conflict.

Having my daughter with me 80% of the time was a blessing. It gave me more power than I had realised. I used that power thoughtfully, always prioritising my daughter's well-being over his attempts to create chaos. But just as importantly, I made my peace a priority. My daughter didn't need two parents consumed by conflict. She needed stability and calm, and I tried to provide that, sometimes successfully or not.

Dealing with my ex was one of the most challenging aspects of my journey. Still, it also taught me invaluable lessons about boundaries, emotional resilience, and the power of self-control. By understanding who he was and how he was projecting his faults and insecurities onto me, by refusing to engage in his drama, and by setting clear boundaries, I reclaimed my peace. I created a healthier environment for myself and my daughter. It wasn't easy, and it took time, but in the end, it was worth every effort to protect my sanity and prioritise what truly mattered.

WHAT I KNOW NOW

1. THE TRUTH ABOUT NARCISSISTS AND SELF-WORTH: If there's a narcissist in your life, chances are your self-worth and confidence have already taken a massive hit. Narcissists seem to have an uncanny ability to sense when someone is struggling with self-doubt. They thrive on control, manipulation, and the chaos they create, weaving things like gaslighting into their everyday interactions. Their power grows by making others feel small, insignificant, and dependent.

When I agreed to marry my ex-husband, I was riddled with insecurities—especially about my appearance. My self-esteem was so fragile that his sweet words and compliments felt like a lifeline. I was too caught up in my need for validation to see through the facade.

For years, I lived in that haze, believing his words while ignoring the ways he subtly added to my insecurities. At first, his charm felt comforting, even healing. But over time, I saw how his validation was like a drug—something I needed more and more and something he gave off less and less, quietly stripping away the little confidence I had left.

It wasn't until I began rebuilding myself, piece by piece, that I saw the truth. Overcoming my insecurities gave me clarity. I started seeing the patterns—the ways he manipulated situations, created drama, and used my vulnerability as a weapon. His words weren't a lifeline; they were chains.

I've learned that true confidence doesn't come from someone else's approval. It comes from within, acknowledging my worth without needing anyone to validate it. ßHealing from the damage caused by a narcissist is a long journey, but it's also one of rediscovery. I've learned that my worth was never theirs to define—it was mine to reclaim.

2. WHAT LIES BENEATH THE FACADE: Contrary to what it may seem, a narcissist doesn't truly love themselves. They often carry very little love for who they are. On the surface, they present an image of being high and mighty—confident, self-assured, even untouchable. But underneath that carefully curated mask lies a deep well of insecurity and self-doubt.

In my ex-husband's case, he was running from his own identity. He wasn't comfortable with his background, with being Indian, or with the parts of himself that made him who he was. Everything he did seemed like an attempt to hide or cover up those parts of himself. Whether it was through material success, charm, or arrogance, it was all a smokescreen to avoid facing his reflection.

Looking back, I can see how his insecurities bled into our relationship. Instead of facing his struggles, he projected them onto me, fuelling my doubts to silence his own. This painful truth has taught me something invaluable: how someone treats you often has more to do with their own struggles than your worth.

14

UNAPOLOGETICALLY ME: THE WOMAN I HAVE BECOME

"Be free.
Be you—completely and unapologetically.
The gifts you carry within you
are not meant to be hidden;
they are meant to shine
and be shared with the world in this lifetime."

Throughout my life, my identity has been a story of transformation. As a young girl, I often felt invisible. I was the chubby, dark child who hid in the shadows, believing that if no one noticed me, I'd be safe from judgment or pain. I would sit quietly in the corner, silencing my voice, thinking invisibility was my shield. But deep down, the silence wasn't comforting—it was suffocating.

Then came the rebellious teenager who refused to let anyone dictate who I should be. I broke the rules and defied expectations, not out of spite but because I was desperate to carve out a space where I could exist as *myself*. I didn't want to fit into anyone's box. I was loud, fierce, and untamed, but even in my rebellion, I searched for the version of myself that felt real and whole.

As I stepped into adulthood, the reality of life hit me harder than I could have ever imagined. I became the woman who trusted and loved deeply, only to be betrayed most devastatingly. My marriage, built on dreams and hope, crumbled before my eyes. I was left broken, carrying the weight of betrayal, rejection, and an overwhelming loneliness. As a single mother, I was responsible for raising my daughter, managing a household, and rebuilding a life from the wreckage. Each day felt like a battle, and I didn't recognise the woman staring back at me in the mirror for a long time.

Through tears, sleepless nights, and countless moments of doubt, I slowly rediscovered myself. Now, I stand here—no longer hiding, seeking approval, and no longer apologising for who I am. I am unapologetically and gloriously me. Yes, I am still a dark-skinned, chubby girl, a single mother, and unapologetically myself.

I've walked through the fires of heartbreak and rejection and emerged stronger, wiser, and more grounded. My self-worth no longer depends on the approval or validation of others. It comes from within—a powerful, unshakeable force that knows its value. I've learned to be the gatekeeper of my life, deciding who gets to stay and who doesn't. My peace is my power, and I guard it fiercely.

For the first time, I see myself as beautiful—not in how society defines beauty, but in how I carry my strength, resilience, and love. Beauty is how I laugh with my daughter and dance around the living room, singing, "I'm sexy, and I know it." Those moments are pure joy, free from shame or judgment. I want her to see that beauty is not about fitting into society's mould. It's about loving yourself exactly as you are and embracing every part of your journey.

Solitude no longer scares me. In the quiet, I've found healing. Alone with my thoughts, I've uncovered clarity about who I am, what I need, and the life I want to create. I've learned that other people's triggers and insecurities are not my responsibility. Their actions and words reflect their own wounds, and I've stopped carrying burdens that were never mine to bear.

Today, my journey is one of healing and growth. I no longer chase dramatic transformations. Instead, I focus on the small, intentional steps I take daily. These subtle shifts create ripples of change in my life and in the lives of those I love. By healing myself, I'm healing the world around me—one small act at a time.

I no longer define myself by my roles—the invisible girl, the rebellious teenager, the broken woman. *I am whole because of my scars, not despite them.* They are a testament to my strength, to the battles I've fought and won. I've embraced the light and the shadow within me, knowing that true power comes from accepting and loving all of myself.

As I move forward, I feel a deep sense of purpose. This journey isn't just about me—it's about leaving a legacy of resilience, love, and empowerment. I want my story to be a light for others, a reminder that no matter how dark life gets, there is always a way to rise.

I am the woman I was always meant to be—strong, bold, and unapologetically me.

15

I CAN SEE CLEARLY NOW

*"If you believe it will work out, you will see opportunities.
If you believe it won't you will see obstacles"*

- Dr. Wayne Dyer

A. IT ALL BEGINS WITH YOU: THE MOST IMPORTANT RELATIONSHIP

If I had to distil everything I've learned into a single truth, it's this: my relationship with myself defines the path that shapes my Life.

The most important relationship I will ever have is the one with myself. I have always been by my side—through every high, low, challenge, and triumph—and I'm the only one who will stay with me until the very end. No one else can walk this journey with me in the same way, and no one else has the power to define my worth except me.

As I began to reflect on my Life, I understood that every other relationship I have—whether with a partner, family, friends, or colleagues—reflects my relationship with myself. How I treat myself sets the tone for how others treat me. I attract kind people if I believe the world is a kind place. If I believe the world is dangerous, I tend to encounter those who harm me. What I think and believe about myself shapes how I experience everything. Ultimately, every experience I have reflects my relationship with myself.

When my ex left, I had my first "AHA" moment: I never truly respected or loved myself. I had allowed myself to accept mistreatment, and it shouldn't have been a surprise when he didn't respect or love me either.

The same went for my relationship with my in-laws. There was a lack of empathy, but that was because I wasn't showing empathy toward myself. I had neglected my own needs and feelings for so long that I couldn't expect others to care for me in the way I needed. This was not their fault—it simply reflected how little I valued my well-being.

I also started noticing patterns in other relationships. My mum often complained that I didn't support her enough, and after marriage, my husband would say the same. These complaints were not just about them—they were the universe's way of showing me that I wasn't supporting myself. I wasn't prioritising my needs and desires, and that lack of self-support showed up in my relationships with others.

I now teach people how to treat me by how I treat myself. If I don't have healthy boundaries and let people walk all over me, then I am teaching them that it's okay to treat me that way. But when I love myself enough to set boundaries, I stop people from taking advantage of me. Boundaries aren't walls to keep people out; they are guidelines to protect my energy, my time, and my heart.

Even my relationship with food reflects how I see myself. On days when I feel down, I often turn to unhealthy food as a way to cope because, deep down, I don't feel worthy of taking care of myself. But when I am in self-love, I am more mindful of what I put into my body because I know I deserve nourishment and care.

At my lowest, when I struggled with low self-confidence, I attracted a narcissist into my Life. Even after he hurt me deeply, I begged him to stay. But as I rebuilt my confidence, I found the strength to walk away. I no longer accepted behaviour that disrespected me because I had finally learned to respect myself.

I also realised something powerful: how I speak to myself is often harsher than how I would ever talk to another person—even if they hurt me. Our inner dialogue can be the most cruel and judgmental voice we hear, yet it's the voice we listen to most often. We must learn to value and appreciate the child within us, the human part that longs to be seen, heard, loved, and respected—not scolded or devalued. The healing begins when we treat ourselves with the kindness and compassion we would offer someone we genuinely care about. It all starts with you.

"Life is a mirror
If you smile, it smiles back
If you frown, it frowns back"

B. LIFE IS ALL ABOUT MEANINGS AND EMOTIONS

Life is not just about what happens to us; it's about the meanings we give to those events, people, and situations. These meanings shape the emotions we feel, and those emotions, in turn, define how we experience Life.

Two people can experience the same situation and walk away with entirely different experiences simply because of the meanings they attach to it. Some over-romanticise Life, turning even small challenges into overwhelming dramas in their minds. And then, some take Life in stride, embracing each moment with grace and acceptance.

We are the storytellers of our own lives. The meanings we create are not just reactions to events—they are the framework through which we interpret the world. And the emotions that stem from those meanings act as our compass, influencing the choices we make and the paths we take.

For example, when I was called chubby, it meant just that - I was chubby. But in my head, I made it mean I was ugly, which gave the word 'chubby' a different meaning, and so many negative emotions got attached to it. And I carried those emotions with me for most of my Life, shying away from relationships, not showing up and attracting the wrong people.

For much of my Life, I saw myself as a victim. Every setback felt like a punishment, every hardship a personal failure. But when I changed the meaning of my experiences—when I stopped seeing myself as someone life happened *to* and began seeing myself as someone with inherent value—everything shifted. Challenges became less of a burden and became opportunities to learn, grow, and become stronger.

The relationships in my Life also transformed. When I stopped over-thinking and giving meaning to other people's words, I could show up authentically and connect with the right kind of tribe.

The beauty of Life is that the power to rewrite our stories is always in our hands. When we change the meaning of our circumstances, we can transform the emotions they bring. A failure can become a stepping stone, a loss can become a lesson, and an ending can become a new beginning.

Life has taught me this: the meanings we give are the seeds of our emotional world, and those emotions shape the garden of our lives. We can choose to water the seeds of hope, love, and resilience or dwell on fear, regret, and resentment. The choice is ours.

Ultimately, Life is a dance between meanings and emotions. And when we learn to choose meanings that empower us and emotions that elevate us, we create a life filled with joy, purpose, and peace.

"Change the way you look at things, and the thing you look at changes" - Dr. Wayne Dyer.

C. LIFE IS HAPPENING TO SHAPE ME, NOT BREAK ME

From the moment I took my first breath, Life has been my greatest teacher. Every step, every challenge, every triumph has been a lesson leading me closer to understanding who I truly am. Life has given me challenges so I can overcome them and truly understand my potential and who I am. Looking back, I can see how each experience, even the painful ones, has played a vital role in shaping me.

For a long time, I lived in a constant state of complaining. "Why me? Why is this happening to me?" became my mantra. When my papa passed away while I was still young, I saw myself as a victim of fate. When my mom decided to move to a new city, I felt abandoned and left out. When work got tough, it felt like the weight of the entire world was on my shoulders. And when my ex decided to walk away, my world completely fell apart.

With every challenge—and there were far too many—I wanted to give up. I wanted to run away from it all and sometimes even questioned if Life was worth living. To make it worse, the people I relied on the most, the ones I thought would stand by me, were often the first to leave. This left me feeling isolated, misunderstood, and unloved.

But now, as I reflect, I see the truth I couldn't see then—I was never truly alone. The universe, in its quiet, mysterious way, was always there. It was present in the stillness, patiently guiding me through every heartbreak, every setback, and every storm. Those moments of deep pain and isolation weren't meant to destroy me; they were Life's way of shaping me. Each hardship chiselled away my fears, doubts, and insecurities, slowly revealing the strength, courage, and resilience that had always been within me.

I now see clearly that every moment, whether filled with joy or pain, was part of a greater plan—not to defeat me but to awaken me to my true potential. Each hardship was a call to grow stronger, rise above my circumstances, and uncover the depths of my spirit. Life wasn't punishing me when I was at my lowest; it was preparing me for something far greater than I could imagine.

The universe has always been on my side, even when I couldn't feel its presence. It has been a quiet, steady companion, weaving lessons into every challenge and reminding me of my inner strength. Through pain, I've found compassion. Through struggles, I've discovered resilience. And through it all, I've uncovered a purpose that feels uniquely mine to embrace.

Life didn't shape me by making the path easy; it shaped me by pushing me to find my strength. Today, as I reflect on every step I've taken—every heartbreak, triumph, and tear—I trust they were all part of a journey I was meant to walk.

In the spiritual realm, Life is simply dealing with the cards I chose for this lifetime. I chose my parents, my family, and the challenges that came with them—not as punishments but as opportunities to grow and remember my true essence.

It hasn't been easy, but it has been worth every step. Life isn't here to break me but to build me into the person I was always meant to be.

D. PAIN TRAVELS THROUGH GENERATIONS

Pain is a persistent traveller, weaving its way silently through generations, waiting for someone brave enough to confront it. Unintentionally, it is handed down—grandparents to parents, parents to children—like an invisible, unspoken inheritance. For so many, the only way they knew to deal with pain was to hide it, suppress it, and pretend it didn't exist. Talking about it felt dangerous, as though naming it might unleash emotions too overwhelming to bear. But pain doesn't fade when ignored. It lingers, hovering in the corners of our lives, waiting for someone to see it, feel it, and release it truly.

As I look back on my family, I can clearly see the threads of un-acknowledged pain. My mum lost her husband far too young, leaving her to shoulder the enormous task of raising three children alone. The grief of losing her partner, compounded by the uncertainty of a future without him, left her emotionally vulnerable. She longed for the support and validation of her brothers or family members, trying to fill the void her husband's absence had left. Her pain became a silent weight she carried—a dependence born of insecurity and loneliness, though she rarely spoke of it.

Then, Life presented me with a strikingly similar wound. My husband didn't die, but he chose to leave, and the impact was no less profound. Like my mum, I found myself facing the world alone, raising my daughter amidst the chaos of broken families. The loneliness was sharp, the sense of abandonment deep. I struggled to find my footing, just as my mum had. The parallel was undeniable—her pain had echoed through time, finding its way to me in a different form.

This is how generational pain works. It mutates and adapts, appearing in new contexts but always rooted in the same unresolved emotions. It's not just a family story; it's a cycle that repeats until someone chooses to break it. That choice is mine.

By committing to healing myself, I am doing more than addressing my own struggles—I am rewriting the narrative for my daughter. I am facing the loneliness, insecurity, and wounds of the past so she doesn't have to carry them forward. My healing isn't just for me; it's for her and the generations that will follow.

I want my daughter to know that she is never truly alone. She is deeply loved, supported, and worthy of a life filled with healthy, fulfilling relationships. I want her to believe in her strength, to trust that she doesn't need to depend on someone else to feel whole and to know that her worth is intrinsic.

By facing my pain, I honour the struggles of those who came before me while choosing to end the cycle with me. I am listening to the pain, allowing it to be seen and heard, and finally letting it go. My greatest hope is that the legacy I leave isn't one of inherited wounds but of resilience, love, and freedom. My daughter will inherit not the unspoken burdens of the past but the unshakable truth that she is enough, just as she is.

E. THE BATTLE WAS ALWAYS WITHIN

Looking back now, I see it clearly—my Life was never indeed about "them." It was never about my mother, my ex-husband, or anyone else I once believed was the source of my pain. Every struggle, every conflict, and every moment of rebellion wasn't directed at the world around me but was a mirror reflecting a deeper battle within myself. The real fight was never with them—it was always with me.

For years, I told myself a story that my unhappiness, my struggles, and my frustrations were because of others. I blamed Life for being unfair and the people in it for not meeting my expectations. I spent countless nights in tears, drowning in anger and sadness, convinced that the world was against me. But as time passed, I realised something profound: the world wasn't my enemy. My resistance to facing the truth within myself was.

I was holding onto old wounds, tightly gripping pain that had long outlived its purpose. Pain had become my comfort, as paradoxical as it sounds. Letting it go felt too vulnerable, too risky, like losing a part of myself I'd come to know so intimately. Even though it hurt, I clung to it because it was familiar.

One night, as I sat alone, replaying another painful memory, a wave of sadness and anger swept over me, the same feelings I thought I had left behind. I found myself asking, "Why does this still hurt? Why can't I move on?" And in that moment, the answer revealed itself like a whisper: I hadn't healed the parts of me that felt unworthy, unloved, and abandoned. I had spent so long looking outward, trying to fix the people and situations around me, when the truth was that the healing I needed had to come from within.

It became clear: the only person I was genuinely fighting was myself. The battle wasn't about changing others or forcing circumstances to align with my desires. It was about learning to accept and love myself—even the parts that felt broken. The battle was never about convincing others to tell me I was beautiful; it was about me seeing my beauty. It was never about my husband or anyone else assuring me that I was enough; it was about genuinely believing, "I am enough."

The turning point came when I began to give new meaning to the stories I had told myself for years. Instead of letting words or actions define me negatively, I created empowering emotions around them. Slowly but surely, I realised that the strength I had been searching for outside had been within me all along.

The battle was mine—not to win or lose, but to transform. It wasn't about defeating the parts of me that resisted change but about embracing them with compassion and guiding them toward growth. True peace, I've learned, doesn't come from fixing the world around you. It comes from making peace with yourself and accepting your flaws, scars, and journey as part of the whole.

Today, as I continue on this path of self-healing, my intention is to keep becoming a better version of myself—a little better, a little wiser—from whom I was yesterday. *This is the journey to 'Being you' as the best version of yourself.*

Each step brings me closer to the quiet strength that comes from within, the kind that says, "*I am enough. I am whole. And I am free.*»

F. CONSISTENCY IS THE KEY

I now understand that healing is not a straight path but a journey full of twists, turns, and unexpected detours. For the first 35 years of my Life, I was shaped by patterns and behaviours that no longer align with who I strive to be. A decade of healing cannot erase those deeply ingrained habits overnight. Despite all the lessons I've learned, I still find myself slipping back into old ways. The triggers remain, and the pull to react as I once did can still feel familiar and strong.

Even though I've gained the wisdom to understand my ex, myself, and the dynamics of our relationship, there are moments when the old me resurfaces. A sharp word, a reminder of the past, or an unresolved memory can still knock me off balance.

Nine years into my healing journey, I've accepted that falling off the horse is part of the process. What matters is not avoiding the fall but finding the strength and support to get back up. My tribe—my friends, my coaches, and the people who remind me of my growth—have been instrumental in helping me stay the course.

Even writing this book tested my resilience. There were moments when old wounds reopened, and the pain became too much to bear. I abandoned the project for months, unable to face the emotions it stirred. It took me nearly a year to complete this book because healing doesn't work on a timeline. It comes in waves—some gentle, some powerful enough to knock you over.

Through this journey, I've learned that consistency is the key. Healing isn't about never falling but how quickly you can rise again. There are days when I feel like all the hard work I've put in myself has led to nothing, where the progress seems invisible. But there are also days when I can see how far I've come—when I can look at my journey and feel pride in the person I'm becoming.

Healing isn't about perfection. It's about persistence. The work is never truly done; maybe it's not meant to be. Life will continue to test me, and I will continue to grow. What matters is not how many times I fall but how committed I am to getting back up, dusting myself off, and trying again.

This journey has taught me to be kinder to myself, to embrace the imperfections, and to trust the process. Every stumble, every pause, and every moment of doubt has been a part of my transformation. As I look ahead, I know the key is not in avoiding the falls but in finding the courage to rise again and again.

16

MASCULINE AND FEMININE ENERGIES

A. STEPPING INTO MASCULINE ENERGY

At the age of 14, the day my father passed away, something shifted within me—something I didn't fully understand at the time. He meant to protect me, guide me, and care for me. His sudden absence left a vast void I instinctively stepped forward to fill. Without realising it, I began to take on the role he once held.

It wasn't a conscious decision—it just happened. Along with my sister, I shouldered the responsibility of managing our lives, supporting my mother, and maintaining the household dynamics. When I hit 17, I went from being a child to a young adult. My heart hardened as I grew determined to shield myself from the pain and uncertainty that had upended our lives.

Since then, I lived as a fiercely independent, sassy, career-focused young woman, navigating the highs and lows of life and, yes, enduring more than my fair share of epic relationship fails. I convinced myself that needing anyone, especially a man, was a sign of weakness. Dependence became my greatest fear, and self-sufficiency became my armour.

By the time I reached my late teens, I had built an impenetrable fortress around myself, one that kept vulnerability and emotional connection firmly on the other side. I told myself I didn't need anyone—I could handle everything alone.

At 17, I made the bold decision to live independently. It was a rebellious act of courage and a reflection of my deep-seated belief that I was the only one I could rely on. The more I leaned into my independence, the more disconnected I became from the nurturing, gentle side of me that longed for connection and love.

I wore my strength like armour, proud of my ability to navigate life on my terms. But beneath the surface, a softer part of me felt unseen, unheard, and unacknowledged.

When I got married, everything shifted again. For the first time in a long time, the parts of me I had buried—the longing to be cared for, the need to be protected, and the desire to feel loved—began to surface. I wanted to soften, let my guard down, and feel safe enough to receive love.

But when my ex-husband didn't immediately step up to provide the emotional support I needed, my walls instinctively came back up. Instead of communicating my needs or permitting myself to feel vulnerable, I retreated to what I knew best: taking control. I took on responsibilities, made decisions, and tried to fix everything in our married life myself. It became a pattern—every time I felt unsupported, I would lean harder into my independence.

A year later, through this personal development journey, I stumbled upon a revelation that changed everything. I learned about masculine and feminine energies—the dynamic forces within us that shape our relationships and inner worlds. It became clear to me how, in my marriage, I had unconsciously leaned heavily into my masculine energy—taking charge, solving problems, and striving for control.

I often debated with myself: did my independence make him not step up, or did his inability to step up push me back into being independent? This question lingered in my mind for years.

B. UNDERSTANDING MASCULINE AND FEMININE ENERGIES

So, what are masculine and Feminine Energies?

A delicate balance of masculine and feminine energies is at the core of every individual and relationship. These energies, often misunderstood as being tied to gender, are universal forces that exist in everyone, regardless of whether you identify as male or female. They represent two distinct ways of being in the world—dynamic (masculine) and magnetic (feminine).

MASCULINE ENERGY is dynamic, action-oriented, and focused on doing. It thrives on structure, direction, and purpose. The energy drives us to set goals, take risks, and create order out of chaos. Masculine energy is about providing, protecting, and achieving. It's the force that says, *"I can do this; I will make this happen."*

FEMININE ENERGY, on the other hand, is magnetic, nurturing, and focused on being. It's fluid, intuitive, and creative. Feminine energy invites receptivity, connection, and flow. It's about feeling, surrendering, and creating a natural space for things to unfold. Feminine energy whispers, *"I trust what I desire will come to me."*

Both these energies are essential for every human, and their dance creates harmony in our lives and relationships. Problems in relationships arise, however, when there's an imbalance—when both partners are playing in one energy or when they suppress one energy in favour of the other.

C. HOW MASCULINE ENERGY ERODED OUR CONNECTION

The imbalance in my marriage stemmed, in part, from me operating predominantly in my masculine energy—independent, self-sufficient, and always in control. It wasn't intentional; it was a survival mechanism I had adopted in my father's absence.

From the very beginning, I instinctively took charge. When my husband didn't step up in ways I expected or needed, I took matters into my own hands. If something needed to be done, I made it happen. While my actions came from a place of strength and capability, they carried unintended consequences.

It wasn't just about the tasks I took on—it was the message I unknowingly sent. By showing him I could handle everything, I inadvertently made him complacent. The more responsibilities I shouldered, the more he let go. I created a dynamic where he felt unneeded by proving I didn't need him.

This pattern taught him to rely on me and drained me. Deep down, I yearned to fall back, to feel supported, and to allow myself to receive. But when I hit breaking points, I didn't ask for help or show vulnerability. Instead, I pushed myself harder or turned to arguments, reinforcing the cycle.

I stepped in to manage his business when he grew weary of it. While he knew I was capable, it hurt his ego. So, whilst I thought I was supporting him, I was subtly pushing him out of spaces where he could have felt like being the giver, the protector and the provider.

My impatience, fear of letting go of control, and hesitation to rely on anyone else built an invisible wall between us. The more I stepped into my masculine energy, the more he retreated. My financial independence only added to the imbalance. When my salary surpassed his, the dynamic of give-and-receive—a cornerstone of healthy relationships—tilted further.

In my fierce independence, I unintentionally left no room for him to feel needed. But here's the truth: men are wired to give, just as women are wired to receive. It's an intuitive balance. Yet, I wasn't in my receiving energy, and he wasn't in his giving energy.

Over time, the imbalance became a chasm. As he lost his sense of purpose in the relationship, he withdrew. The more he withdrew, the more independent I became. Eventually, the distance between us grew too wide.

When he found someone who stroked his ego, someone who allowed him to feel like a man again—someone who gave him space to step into his masculine energy—he chose her.

I'll never know for sure, but I believe he stopped feeling like the man in our relationship. My inability to let go and his inability to step up created a dynamic that neither of us knew how to escape. Ultimately, it wasn't just love that failed us; it was the loss of balance and the inability to meet each other where we needed to be.

D. RESTORING HARMONY WITHIN MYSELF

After my marriage ended, I began to reflect deeply on how my dominant masculine energy had shaped my life and relationships. For years, I believed that being strong, independent, and self-reliant was the only way to navigate the world. While this approach had its strengths, it also left me disconnected from a softer, more vulnerable part of myself—the part that longed for love, support, and genuine connection.

Healing meant learning to embrace and restore balance by reconnecting with my feminine energy—the energy of trust, creativity, and openness. At first, this felt incredibly unnatural. Vulnerability frightened me, and trusting others felt impossible after years of self-reliance. But I knew I had to unlearn old patterns if I truly wanted to heal and grow. Here's where I began:

1. KNOW MYSELF: Knowing yourself is the first step in any healing process. Self-awareness is the foundation of growth. I had no idea how deeply I was living in my masculine energy until it was pointed out to me. Once I became aware, I could consciously begin making changes. Regular self-reflection allowed me to recognise patterns in my thoughts, feelings, and actions. I used powerful tools like journalling and meditation to help increase my self-awareness.

2. ALLOWING MYSELF TO RECEIVE: As I grew more self-aware, I began to notice a recurring pattern: I was always a giver, never a receiver. Giving came naturally to me; it felt safe, even empowering. But receiving? That made me deeply uncomfortable. Somewhere along the way, my fierce independence had turned into a barrier. I stopped asking for help, even when things became overwhelming. It was as if admitting I needed support was a sign of weakness.

My coach saw through this and gave me a task: to practice receiving. She arranged for my friends to take me out and insisted I let them pay. She encouraged me to go on dates and allow the man to pay, even if I knew there was no romantic connection. At first, it felt unnatural, almost wrong. I wanted to resist, to insist that I could handle everything alone.

But this exercise wasn't about the money or the gestures but about breaking down the walls I had built. It forced me to confront my discomfort, let go of control, and allow others to show up for me. Over time, I started to understand that receiving didn't make me less capable—it made me more human.

Although I've come a long way, I still struggle to ask for help or accept support. Those old patterns don't disappear overnight. But now, when I notice myself resisting, I pause and remind myself that allowing others to give is not just a gift to me; it's also a gift to them.

3. EMBRACE VULNERABILITY: I don't always have to be strong. True strength lies in allowing myself to be open, to share my fears, and to lean on others when I need support. In trying to appear strong all the time, I was unintentionally depriving my friends, family, and loved ones of the joy and privilege of being there for me.

Vulnerability has shown me the power of emotional connection and intimacy. By letting the people around me see my true self—good and messy—I've created more authentic and fulfilling relationships.

Being vulnerable is especially important in romantic relationships. It allows my partner to be a part of my life, not just an observer from the outside. Vulnerability opens the door for them to support me, understand me on a deeper level, and share the emotional journey together.

Through this process, I've discovered a beautiful balance between strength and softness. And in that balance, I've found peace and a more profound sense of connection to myself and others.

4. DANCE MY WAY INTO LIFE: As a child, I loved dancing. Whether I was studying or just passing time, I could always be found grooving to some music. But dancing faded into the background as life got busier and more demanding. It wasn't until later that I realised how vital dance was to embrace my feminine energy, and one of the best ways to do that was through movement.

Dancing, as simple as it may seem, became my way back to my femininity. Allowing myself to let go of physical rigidity and flow freely to the rhythm of the music helped me reconnect with a side of me that had been dormant for too long. It wasn't just about the movement but about feeling sensual, vibrant, and alive.

Dance became my way of releasing control, letting go, and embracing the natural flow of life. Through dancing, I found a powerful way to embody my feminine energy, reminding me that life isn't always about being in control but about feeling the rhythm and enjoying the dance.

As I started to understand this balance of energies, I understood that being in my feminine energy didn't mean I was weak or incapable. It meant I could be strong and soft at the same time. I didn't need to carry everything alone. I could allow others to give, help, and support me.

Restoring the balance between my masculine and feminine energy didn't just heal me—it also changed how I approached all my relationships. I became more patient, open, and willing to let go of control. I learned that true strength lies in knowing when to step forward and when to step back, lead, and lean.

This balance is a practice—something I'm still learning and growing into every day. But now, I know I don't have to choose between independence and vulnerability. I can have both. To attract driven-confident, relationship-ready men, I must lean into my magnetic energy and express it. A man must connect to my feline side to feel romantically attracted to me.

17

DATING AFTER DIVORCE

Dating after divorce has been a journey of twists, turns, and emotional challenges. When I first separated, the well-meaning advice from friends and family to "get out there" and meet new people only made me feel more isolated. I wasn't ready. I was broken, my confidence shattered, and the thought of anyone wanting to date me felt like an impossible dream.

In those early days, the idea of dating terrified me. I was still healing, still mending from the pain of betrayal and the destruction of my self-esteem. The thought of being vulnerable again seemed daunting. But, as time passed and I began diving deeper into my healing, I started to feel like I was shifting emotionally.

I could feel the changes inside me. Slowly, I began to rebuild my confidence. I started to feel comfortable in my own skin again, and a new sense of beauty emerged. There was one moment that stood out vividly. Someone asked me, "What do you like about yourself?" without hesitation, I answered, "Oh, a lot! It's a long list; where should I start?" That response from a woman who had once been lost, insecure, and broken amazed me. I had come so far from the person my ex had left behind. I even started taking selfies—something I would have avoided at all costs.

With this newfound confidence, I decided to try online dating. I created a profile torn between excitement and nervousness. It was an interesting experience, to say the least.

The reality of dating was foreign to me—I'd only ever had one relationship, and that was with my ex-husband. So, I felt like a fish out of water, unsure where to begin. At first, the attention I received was anything but encouraging. Casual talk about sex and requests for nude pictures were disturbingly familiar. It was clear that the next steps with these men weren't what I was looking for.

As I continued working on my self-worth, I shifted my approach. I made it clear that I wasn't interested in those types of conversations, but I soon found myself attracting a different kind of attention: men who lacked confidence. Some were so unsure of themselves that it was impossible even to have a meaningful conversation. I found myself going on some genuinely bizarre dates where men looked nothing like their photos, and red flags were everywhere.

With time and experience, I started to recognise these red flags more clearly. But just as I began to get better at identifying what wasn't right, I ran into another issue. The type of men I attracted now were emotionally scarred, hesitant to commit, and often wanted everything without the label—no strings attached. I understood the term "Friends with Benefits" in a way I never had before.

Over the course of a couple of years, I gained a wealth of experience in the dating world. The "good girl" I once was had faded, replaced by someone more self-aware and better equipped to navigate the complexities of dating. I started to notice my own growth and the traumas, insecurities, and unresolved issues that others carried. It became clear that many men I encountered weren't ready for a real connection.

I found myself rejecting men more quickly as I began to see how much emotional baggage they were carrying. Most of them didn't even make it past the initial conversation, and even fewer made it to a video call. And only a select few ever reached the point of "let's meet." Dating after divorce was a complex journey, but each step brought me closer to understanding myself, my needs, and what I truly wanted in a partner.

There were a few good encounters where I thought something might work out, but in the end, nothing ever did. Not because I wasn't desirable but because I had raised my standards. I had learned that I no longer had to settle for anything less than what I knew I deserved. It wasn't that I couldn't find someone who liked me—it was that I couldn't find anyone I liked enough to let into my life.

There was one encounter in particular that left a lasting impression on me. For a while, I thought he could be someone I could build something meaningful with. But after a few months, it became clear that he wasn't ready to offer anything beyond casual dating. By this point, I had learned an essential lesson about feminine energy: women don't settle into their feminine energy because they're asked to or are supposed to. They do so when they feel they can trust a man's words and actions, feel safe and secure in the relationship, and know they're not the only ones carrying the weight of the relationship. In that space of trust and mutual effort, she can soften, disarm herself, and step into her magnetic energy.

I needed him to step up and show me he could be the partner I needed—but he didn't. And I wasn't willing to step down or shrink for any man anymore. So, I let it go.

And so, my dating journey continues. I've learned that I'd much rather be alone than in another toxic relationship. I no longer fear solitude; I embrace it as a space for growth and self-discovery. My worth is no longer tied to being in a relationship but to being true to myself. I'm not just looking for someone to fill a void—I'm looking for a connection that complements the person I've become.

As I navigate this new chapter of life, I do so with clarity and confidence. I know I am whole on my own, and I have faith that the right person will come when the time is right. But until then, I'm content with the journey. I'm savouring the process of rediscovering who I am, what I truly want, and what aligns with me. My heart is open, but it's no longer willing to settle for anything less than what truly serves me. And that, in itself, is a beautiful step forward.

TESTIMONIALS

"As someone who has always been short-tempered and conservative, I never realised how much I needed guidance until my sister Kshama began coaching me. Through her coaching, Kshama helped me confront and overcome my fears, transforming me into a calm and self-loving person. This change didn't just affect my personal life; it also gave me the confidence to grow in my business. Not only have I been able to innovate in my business, but my relationship with our mother has healed, making me feel free and lighter. While we, like any sisters, have our disagreements, when it comes to living my life on my own terms, she truly takes on the role of my elder sister. Kshama has taught me to prioritise myself, something I never thought I could do. Thanks to her, I have learned to love myself and, in turn, become a more loving person to my family. I can't thank her enough for helping me become so self-confident."

— *Tapasya Gupta, Netra Designs*

"I must admit that I was skeptical about how coaching could help me. But my sessions have completely changed my outlook and literally transformed my life in just 12 weeks. I feel more calm, confident, resilient and content with my life."

— *Louise Oliver*

"With coaching I realised that I was giving the power away. I was waiting for permission and by waiting I was making myself small. Kshama made me realise that I have to first take the action, and then the fear will disappear."
— *Gitana Piscikiene*

Printed in Great Britain
by Amazon